FOUR THEORIES OF THE PRESS

FOUR THEORIES
OF THE PRESS

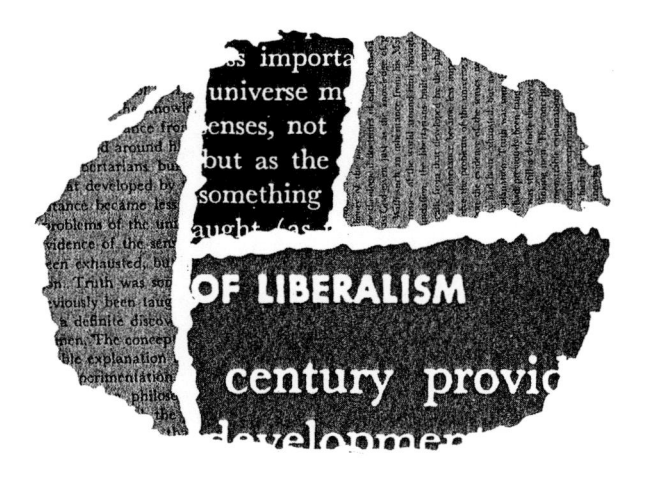

THE AUTHORITARIAN, LIBERTARIAN, SOCIAL RESPONSIBILITY AND
SOVIET COMMUNIST CONCEPTS OF WHAT THE PRESS SHOULD BE AND DO

FRED S. SIEBERT · THEODORE PETERSON · WILBUR SCHRAMM

UNIVERSITY OF ILLINOIS PRESS   Urbana and Chicago

Originally published in a clothbound edition, 1956
© 1956, 1984 by the Board of Trustees of the University of Illinois
Manufactured in the United States of America
P   24   23   22   21

Library of Congress Catalog Card No. 56-11881
ISBN 0-252-72421-6
ISBN 978-0-252-72421-3

These essays were prepared in connection with a study of the social responsibilities of mass communicators which Dr. Schramm conducted for the Department of the Church and Economic Life of the National Council of Churches. The authors are grateful to the Council for releasing these materials for publication apart from the study.

CONTENTS

later
develop

Develop
after

INTRODUCTION

By *press*, in this book, we mean all the media of mass communication, although we shall talk about the printed media oftener than about broadcast or film because the printed media are older and have gathered about them more of the theory and philosophy of mass communication.

In simplest terms the question behind this book is, why is the press as it is? Why does it apparently serve different purposes and appear in widely different forms in different countries? Why, for example, is the press of the Soviet Union so different from our own, and the press of Argentina so different from that of Great Britain?

Partly, of course, these differences reflect the ability of a country to pay for its press, the mechanical ingenuity and resources that can be put behind mass communication, and the relative degree of urbanization which makes the circulation of mass media at once easier and more necessary. Partly, the differences in the press of different countries reflect simply what people do in different places and what their experience leads them to want to read about.

But there is a more basic and important reason for these differences. The thesis of this volume is that the press always takes on the form and coloration of the social and political structures within which it operates. Especially, it reflects the system of social control whereby the relations of individuals and institutions are adjusted. We believe that an understanding of these aspects of society is basic to any systematic understanding of the press.

To see the differences between press systems in full perspective, then, one must look at the social systems in which the press functions. To see the social systems in their true relationship to the press, one has to look at certain basic beliefs and assumptions which the society holds: the nature of man, the nature of society and the state, the relation of man to the state, and the nature of knowledge and truth. Thus, in the last analysis the difference between press systems is one of philosophy, and this book is about the philosophical and political rationales or theories which lie behind the different kinds of press we have in the world today.

Since the beginning of mass communication, in the Renaissance, there have been only two or four basic theories of the press — two or four, that is, according to how one counts them. We have written four essays about them, but have tried to make clear that the latter two "theories" are merely developments and modifications of the first two. The *Soviet Communist* theory is only a development of the much older *Authoritarian* theory, and what we have called the *Social Responsibility* theory is only a modification of the *Libertarian* theory. But because the Soviets have produced something so spectacularly different from older authoritarianism, and something so important to the world today, and because the social responsibility theory road is the apparent direction of development which our own press is now taking, we have thought it better to treat them as four separate theories, meanwhile trying to point out their relationships.

The oldest of these theories is the Authoritarian. It came into being in the authoritarian climate of the late Renaissance, soon after the invention of printing. In that society, truth was conceived to be, not the product of the great mass of people, but of a few wise men who were in a position to guide and direct their fellows. Thus truth was thought to be centered near the center of power. The press therefore functioned *from the top down*. The rulers of the time used the press to inform the people of what the rulers thought they should know and the policies the rulers thought they should support. The Tudors and Stuarts maintained that the press belonged to the office of king and therefore was obligated to support the royal policy. Only by special permission was private ownership of the press permitted, and this permission could be withdrawn any time the obligation to support the royal policies was considered to have been dishonored. Publishing was thus a sort of agreement between power source and publisher, in which the former granted a monopoly right and the latter gave support. But the power source kept the right to set and change policy, the right to license, and in some cases the right to censor. It is obvious that this concept of the press eliminated what has come in our own time to be one of the most common press functions: to check on government.

This theory of the press — the press being a servant of the state responsible for much of its content to the power figures in charge of government at any given moment — was universally accepted in the sixteenth and most of the seventeenth centuries. This concept set the original pattern for most of the national press systems of the world, and still persists. Indeed, as the following chapters will make clear, authoritarian practice is still found to some extent in all parts of the world even though another theory has been accepted, in word if not in deed, by most of the non-Communist nations. But the growth of political democracy and religious freedom, the expansion of free trade and travel, the acceptance of laissez-faire economics, and the general philosophical climate of the Enlightenment, undermined authoritarianism and called for a new concept of the press. This new theory, which was incipient in the late seventeenth century, came into real being in the eighteenth, and flowered in the nineteenth, is what we have called the *Libertarian* theory.

The Libertarian theory reverses the relative position of man and the state as we saw it in the Authoritarian theory. Man is no longer conceived of as a dependent being to be led and directed, but rather as a rational being able to discern between truth and falsehood, between a better and worse alternative, when faced with conflicting evidence and alternative choices. Truth is no longer conceived of as the property of power. Rather, the right to search for truth is one of the inalienable natural rights of man. And where does the press fit into the scheme? The press is conceived of as *a partner in the search for truth*.

In Libertarian theory, the press is not an instrument of government, but rather a device for presenting evidence and arguments on the basis of which the people can check on government and make up their minds as to policy. Therefore, it is imperative that the press be free from government control and influence. In order for truth to emerge, all ideas must get a fair hearing; there must be a "free market place" of ideas and information. Minorities as well as majorities, the weak as well as the strong, must have access to the press. This is the theory of the press which was written into our Bill of Rights.

For two hundred years the United States and Great Britain have maintained this kind of press, almost wholly free of government influence and encouraged to serve as a "Fourth Estate" in the governing process. As we indicated earlier, most other non-Communist countries have given at least lip service to the Libertarian theory of the press. But in our own century there have been currents of change. These currents have taken the form of a new authoritarianism in the Communist countries and a trend toward a new Libertarianism in the non-Communist countries. It is the second of these that we have called, for want of a better name, the *Social Responsibility* theory.

The new Libertarianism received wide publicity in connection with the reports of the Hutchins Commission, but the theory was reflected much earlier by editors and publishers themselves. These men realized that twentieth-century conditions demand of the mass media a new and different kind of social responsibility. This realization came about the time that people began to measure and assess the "communication revolution" through which they were passing.

It was apparent thirty years ago that it was no longer easy to enter the publishing business or to operate a newspaper or a radio station. As these units grew large, their ownership and management came to involve huge amounts of money. No longer was the typical pattern a multiplicity of small media units representing different political viewpoints, from which the reader could select. Now, less than seven per cent of the daily newspaper towns of the United States have competing ownership in the dailies. Three television, four radio networks, three wire services, shape a large part of the information that goes into the American home. In other words the press, as in the old authoritarian days, is falling into the hands of a powerful few. It is true that these new rulers of the press are not, for the most part, political rulers. As a matter of fact, they rigorously protect the press against government. But the very fact that control of the press is so limited puts a new and uneasy power into the hands of media owners and managers. No longer is it easy for the press to be a free market place of ideas, as defined by Mill and Jefferson. As the Commission on Freedom of the Press said, "protection against government is not now enough to guarantee that a man who has something to say shall have a chance to say it. The owners and managers of the press determine which persons, which facts, which versions of these facts, shall reach the public." This uneasiness is the basis of the developing Social Responsibility theory: that the power and near monopoly position of the media impose on them an obligation to be socially responsible, to see that all sides are fairly presented and that the public has enough information to decide; and that if the media do not take on themselves such responsibility it may be necessary for some other agency of the public to enforce it.

Let us say again that the Social Responsibility theory should not be thought of as an abstraction produced by the group of scholars who made up the Hutchins Commission. The theory has been so treated by some factions of the press with which the Hutchins Commission was in bad odor. But all the essentials of this theory were expressed by responsible editors and publishers long before the Commission, and have been stated by other responsible editors and publishers since and quite independently of the Commission. It is a trend, not an academic exercise.

While the Libertarian theory has been wrestling with its own problems and shaping its own destiny, a new and dramatic development of authoritarianism has arisen to challenge it. This is, of course, the *Soviet Communist* theory of the press. Grounded in Marxist determinism and in the harsh political necessity of maintaining the political ascendancy of a party which represents less than ten per cent of the country's people, the Soviet press operates as a tool of the ruling power just as clearly as did the older authoritarianism. Unlike the older pattern, it is state rather than privately owned. The profit motive has been removed, and a concept of positive has been substituted for a concept of negative liberty. Perhaps no press in the history of the world has ever been so tightly controlled, and yet the Soviet spokesmen think of their press as free because it is free to speak the "truth" as the Party sees the truth. The American press is not truly free, the Soviets say, because it is business controlled and therefore not free to speak the Marxist "truth." Thus the two systems line up almost diametrically opposite in their basic tenets, although both use words like freedom and responsibility to describe what they are doing. Our press tries to contribute to the search for truth; the Soviet press tries to convey pre-established Marxist-Leninist-Stalinist truth. We think of the audiences of our press as "rational men," able to choose between truth and falsehood; the Soviets think of theirs as needing careful guidance from caretakers, and to this end the Soviet state sets up the most complete possible safeguards against competing information. We bend over backward to make sure that information and ideas will compete. They bend over backward to make sure that only the line decided upon will flow through the Soviet channels. We say that their press is not free; they say that our press is not responsible.

These are the four theories which have largely determined what kind of press the Western world has had: The Authoritarian theory grounded in centuries of authoritarian political thought from Plato to Machiavelli; the Libertarian, grounded in Milton, Locke, Mill and the Enlightenment; the Social Responsibility, grounded in a communication revolution and in certain behavioristic doubts about the philosophy of the Enlightenment; and the Soviet Communist, grounded in Marx, Lenin, Stalin, and the dictatorship of the Communist Party in the Soviet Union. We shall take up these theories, one by one, in the following pages.

Each of the four chapters that follows represents the individual work, style, and opinion of its author. We have made no attempt to impose a majority viewpoint on any of the moot points discussed in these chapters, although we have talked over among ourselves our papers and our conclusions.

We shall begin, then, with the first theory in point of time, the Authoritarian.

FOUR RATIONALES FOR THE MASS MEDIA

	AUTHORITARIAN	LIBERTARIAN	SOCIAL RESPONSIBILITY	SOVIET-TOTALITARIAN
Developed	in 16th and 17th century England; widely adopted and still practiced in many places	adopted by England after 1688, and in U.S.; influential elsewhere	in U.S. in the 20th century	in Soviet Union, although some of the same things were done by Nazis and Italians
Out of	philosophy of absolute power of monarch, his government, or both	writings of Milton, Locke, Mill, and general philosophy of rationalism and natural rights	writing of W. E. Hocking, Commission on Freedom of Press, and practitioners; media codes	Marxist-Leninist-Stalinist thought, with mixture of Hegel and 19th century Russian thinking
Chief purpose	to support and advance the policies of the government in power; and to service the state	to inform, entertain, sell — but chiefly to help discover truth, and to check on government	to inform, entertain, sell — but chiefly to raise conflict to the plane of discussion	to contribute to the success and continuance of the Soviet socialist system, and especially to the dictatorship of the party
Who has right to use media?	whoever gets a royal patent or similar permission	anyone with economic means to do so	everyone who has something to say	loyal and orthodox party members
How are media controlled?	government patents, guilds, licensing, sometimes censorship	by "self-righting process of truth" in "free market place of ideas," and by courts	community opinion, consumer action, professional ethics	surveillance and economic or political action of government
What forbidden?	criticism of political machinery and officials in power	defamation, obscenity, indecency, wartime sedition	serious invasion of recognized private rights and vital social interests	criticism of party objectives as distinguished from tactics
Ownership	private or public	chiefly private	private unless government has to take over to insure public service	public
Essential differences from others	instrument for effecting government policy, though not necessarily government owned	instrument for checking on government and meeting other needs of society	media must assume obligation of social responsibility; and if they do not, someone must see that they do	state-owned and closely controlled media existing solely as arm of state

THE AUTHORITARIAN

THEORY OF

THE PRESS

FRED S. SIEBERT 1

Of the four theories of the relation of the press to society or to government, the authoritarian has been most pervasive both historically and geographically. It is the theory which was almost automatically adopted by most countries when society and technology became sufficiently developed to produce what today we call the "mass media" of communication. It furnishes the basis for the press systems in many modern societies; even where it has been abandoned, it has continued to influence the practices of a number of governments which theoretically adhere to libertarian principles.

For almost two hundred years after the spread of printing in the western world, the authoritarian theory furnished the exclusive basis for determining the function and relationship of the popular press to contemporary society. The Tudors in England, the Bourbons in France, the Hapsburgs in Spain, in fact practically all western Europe, utilized the basic principles of authoritarianism as the theoretical foundation for their systems of press control. Nor has the application of the theory been limited to the sixteenth and seventeenth centuries. The theory has been the basic doctrine for large areas of the globe in succeeding centuries. It has been consciously or unconsciously adopted in modern times by such diverse national units as

Japan, Imperial Russia, Germany, Spain, and many of the Asiatic and South American governments. One can hazard that the authoritarian doctrine has determined the mass communication pattern for more people over a longer time than any other theory of press control.

All human societies, it seems, possess an inherent capacity to develop systems of social control whereby the relations of individuals and of institutions are adjusted and common interests and desires are secured. As described by W. J. Shepard, "such systems are of two general kinds, those which operate spontaneously and automatically, springing directly from the common sense of right of the community and enforced by sanctions of social pressure, and those which have acquired a definite institutional organization and operate by means of legal mandates enforced by definite penalties. This latter form of social control is government, using the term in its broadest sense" (21:8). The authoritarian theory of press control, as we shall discuss it, is a system of principles which has resulted in the second type of social control described by Shepard. It is a theory under which the press, as an institution, is controlled in its functions and operation by organized society through another institution, government.

BASIC POSTULATES

Since the press as well as other forms of mass communication was introduced into an already highly organized society, its relation to that society was naturally determined by the basic assumptions or postulates which were then furnishing the foundation for social controls. Since most governments of western Europe were operating on authoritarian principles when the popular press emerged, these same principles became the basis for a system of press control.

Any theory of relationship of the mass media of communication to the organized society of which it is a part is determined by certain basic philosophical assumptions (or conclusions, if you wish) about man and the state. For our purposes these areas of assumption can be identified as follows: (1) the nature of man, (2) the nature of society and of the state, (3) the relation of man to the state, and (4) the basic philosophical problem, the nature of knowledge and of truth.

The authoritarian theory of the functions and purposes of organized society accepted certain postulates in those areas. First of all, man could attain his full potentialities only as a member of society. As an individual, his sphere of activity was extremely limited, but as a member of society or of an organized community his ability to achieve his goals was immeasurably increased. Under this assumption, the group took on an importance greater than that of the individual since only through the group could an individual accomplish his purposes.

The theory inevitably developed the proposition that the state, the highest expression of group organization, superseded the individual in a scale of values since without the state the individual was helpless in developing the attributes of a civilized man. The individual's dependence on the state for achieving an advanced civilization appears to be a common ingredient of all authoritarian systems. In and through the state, man achieves his ends; without the state, man remains a primitive being.

The state, then, was essential to the full development of man; that assumption resulted in certain basic conclusions concerning the nature of the state. Aside from its individual constituents, the state became the summation of all desirable attributes. It derived its power to determine ends and methods for achieving those ends through a process not generally capable of complete human analysis. Sometimes it was divine guidance, sometimes it was dependence on superior intellect or on leadership qualities, sometimes it was lack of confidence in any other type of process.

To the more basic philosophical problems of the nature of knowledge and of truth, the authoritarians gave equally categorical answers. Knowledge was discoverable through mental effort. Men differed widely in their ability to utilize mental processes and in their drive to exert mental effort. Since such differences existed, they should be recognized in the social structure. "Wise men" capable of analyzing and synthesizing should become leaders in organized society, or if not leaders, they should at least become the advisors of leaders. Knowledge which is not divinely inspired is acquired through human effort, and this effort can best be channeled for the good of all through the state. Knowledge thus acquired or developed becomes the standard for all members of society and acquires an absolutist aura which makes change undesirable and stability or continuity a virtue in itself. In addition, the authoritarian's theory demanded a unity of intellectual activity since only through unity could the state operate successfully for the good of all. The idealist in the authoritarian camp postulated that this unity would come from the realization of the contribution of each to the society as a whole, while the realists recognized that such unity of thought could in most circumstances be attained only through constant surveillance and control.

PLATO ON AUTHORITARIAN THEORY

Let us now turn to some of the exponents of the authoritarian theory of government. Plato idealized the aristocratic form of government. He was convinced that the nature of man, including his material interests and selfish passions, would tend to degrade government from an aristocracy to timocracy, to oligarchy, to democracy, and finally to tyranny. He thought the state was safe only in the hands of wise men, the magistrates, who are governed by moral authority and who use this authority to keep the baser elements of society in line. Just as the wise man disciplines himself by keeping the impulses of his heart and the greed of his stomach under control by his intellect, so in society the magistrate keeps other classes of members from degenerating into a confused chaos. According to Plato, once authority in a state is equally distributed degeneration sets in.

In line with these basic postulates, Plato conceived the ideal society as one in which the state established and enforced the unity of political and cultural goals. That idea meant rigorous control of opinion and discussion. "Plato wanted to 'co-ordinate' the life of the citizens under a strict cultural code that banned all modes of art and even of opinion not in accord with his own gospel. Very politely, in the *Republic,* he would 'send to another city' all offenders against the rigid rules prescribed for the artist and the philosopher and the poet. With equal politeness, in the *Laws,* he would require poets first to submit their works to the magistrates, who should decide whether they were good for the spiritual health of the citizens" (15:322).

Even Plato's famous teacher, Socrates, could not devise a satisfactory answer to the conflicting demands of lawful authority and freedom of the individual. While insisting on his individual right to deviate from the cultural life of Athens, Socrates recognized the philosophical necessity for obedience to authority. He objected to the rules under which he was convicted for seducing the youth of his city because he thought they were wrong, but he accepted the right of the authorities to enforce those rules however wrong. His only solution was to accept the penalty.

MACHIAVELLI AND LATER WRITERS

Succeeding social and political philosophers who have accepted authoritarian principles in government include such well-known names as Machiavelli, Hobbes, Hegel and Treitschke. Machiavelli, unlike his Greek and Roman predecessors, was unconcerned about the purposes and aims of the state. He was concerned, however, with the means of attaining and maintaining political power. He held a basically pessimistic view of human nature and in his theory would subordinate all other considerations to the principal aim, the security of the state. This was to be achieved by a realistic, nonmoralistic policy on the part of the ruler or the prince. Under such a doctrine, public discussion must necessarily be confined whenever the ruler thought that it threatened the security of his principality. Machiavelli was not too concerned whether the government was a monarchy or a republic (in fact, he indicated that perhaps a republic was superior). But he was convinced that, human nature being what it is, the role of the political leader is to utilize whatever means are necessary to forward the interests of his political unit. His influence on nineteenth-century German and Italian political theorists of national movements has been generally recognized.

Implicit in Machiavelli's writings is the proposition that patriotic grounds justify strict control of the methods of discussion and of mass dissemination of information as the basis for political action. The stability and advance of the state are paramount; individualistic considerations of the citizen are subordinate. (See 3:191-202.)

Thomas Hobbes is perhaps the best-known English philosopher of authoritarianism. Starting from two basic desires in man, freedom from pain and the will to power, Hobbes developed a complete system of political philosophy in which a power to check the individual in the interest of all was essential. The power to establish and maintain order and peace is sovereign. It is not subject to private opinions on whether or not its specific actions are reasonable, since its establishment with competence to decide disputes is the prime dictate of reason.

As Catlin has pointed out, Hobbes' theories led to this conclusion: "Doctrines of the division of sovereignty, the subjection of the sovereign to law or its restriction in action by the opinion and conscience of individuals are false. Very wealthy men or guilds and corporations with claims to a measure of autonomy, common lawyers who place custom above the living sovereign power, and churches which claim a spiritual allegiance rivaling that of the sovereign are threats to the sovereign, to civic peace and to reason" (4:395). Hobbes' theories about the nature of the state and man's relation to the state tended to justify many of the authoritarian policies of seventeenth-century governments. Although his greatest work, the *Leviathan,* was attacked by both Royalists and Cromwellians, and by both Anglicans and Puritans, it has been cited to justify many of the arbitrary acts by governments in succeeding centuries.

Georg Hegel, the German philosopher, has been considered the principal exponent of the political theory of authoritarianism in modern times, and to him have been attributed the genesis of both modern Communism and Fascism. The following short passage cited from Hegel is considered one of the vital texts in European thought. As Alfred Zimmern points out, "every word is pregnant . . . and they trail with them a cloud of memories from the philosophical speculation of the past, from Plato and Aristotle onwards" (28:xvii).

Wrote Hegel:

The State is embodied Morality. It is the ethical spirit which has clarified itself and has taken substantial shape as Will, a Will which is manifest before the world, which is self-conscious and knows its purposes and carries through that which it knows to the extent of its knowledge. Custom and Morality are the outward and visible form of the inner essence of the State; the self-consciousness of the individual citizen, his knowledge and activity, are the outward and visible form of the indirect existence of the State. The self-consciousness of the individual finds the substance of its freedom in the attitude of the citizen, which is the essence, purpose, and achievement of its self-consciousness.

The State is Mind, *per se.* This is due to the fact that it is the embodiment of the substantial Will, which is nothing else than the individual self-consciousness conceived in its abstract form and raised to the universal plane. This substantial and massive unity is an absolute and fixed end in itself. In it freedom attains to the maximum of its rights: but at the same time the State, being an end in itself, is provided with the maximum of rights over against the individual citizens, whose highest duty it is to be members of the State (28:3).

Translating his basic principles into the field of communication and the participation of citizens in public decisions, Hegel ridicules the notion that "all should participate in the business of the state." The individual needs to be informed about and concerned with public problems only as a member of a social class, group, society or organization but not as a member of the state. Freedom, in the Hegelian sense, meant freedom of the individual to know that he is not free but that his actions are determined by history, by society and above all by the Absolute Idea which finds its highest manifestation in the state.

The notion that true freedom is freedom within the state rather than freedom from the state was developed more fully by the German political philosopher and historian, Heinrich von Treitschke, both in his little pamphlet on *Freedom* and in his later monumental work *Politics.* Taking a dim view of democracies in general and the democracies of Switzerland and the United States in particular, Treitschke concluded that the rule of the majority was no guarantee that either political freedom or social liberty would survive. The state, in the ordinary evolution of history, is the great individual; what matters is its freedom and life. And like Nietzsche, with whom he generally disagreed, he concluded as an historian that the hero or leader who headed the state could make the greatest contribution to the welfare of its citizens.

Numerous other social and political philosophers since Plato have espoused, directly or indirectly, the doctrine of authoritarianism. Among them can be counted Jean Jacques Rousseau with his ideas of a nonhereditary monarchy, Thomas Carlyle and his hero theories, Bernard Bosenquet with his emphasis on the determinate function of state-community, and the more recent Ernst Troeltsch, who has summarized the German conception of freedom.

FASCIST AUTHORITARIANISM

By no stretch of the imagination can either Mussolini or Hitler be classed as political philosophers. Nevertheless, both their published statements and their actions indicate a continuation in a perverted form of the doctrines of authoritarianism, and their treatment of the mass media was entirely consistent with the basic principle of absolutism. As described by Catlin,

The Mussolini doctrine involves stress on this notion of achievement through force, struggle, danger; the rejection of pacifism; the violent rejection of liberalism and toleration; the organization of the masses through an elite or vanguard, leading and dominating a popular movement and the rejection of internationalism, and the substitution of "nation" based on the middle class, the "class" meaning proletariat . . . [and] emphasizing the importance of the community as the matrix of the full moral life; and identifying this society with the coercive Modern State (or armed and organized Nation) (3:719).

The supremacy of the state under Fascism is exemplified in the idea of a "corporate state" which was the visible expression of the primacy of the state over the economic and social groups within the nation. Although allied with private enterprise in preserving the capitalistic order, the corporate state was based on a theory of interventionism in both economic and cultural affairs.

Said Mussolini: "Fascism combats the whole complex system of democratic ideology, and repudiates it, whether in its theoretical premises or in its practical application. Fascism denies that the majority, by the simple fact that it is a majority, can direct human society; it denies that numbers alone can govern by means of a periodical consultation, and it affirms the immutable, beneficial, and fruitful inequality of mankind, which can never be permanently leveled through the mere operation of a mechanical process such as universal suffrage" (16:303-04).

Adolph Hitler, more than any other exponent of authoritarianism, expressed the theory of the Fascist or totalitarian State in terms of a composite theory of truth and propaganda. Truth for the German Nazis was "our truth — truth for us" — in short, that which would advance the interests and solidarity of the German state.

The following is an oft-quoted excerpt from *Mein Kampf* (9:76-77):

All propaganda should be popular and should adapt its intellectual level to the receptive ability of the least intellectual of those whom it is desired to address. Thus it must sink its mental elevation deeper in proportion to the numbers of the mass whom it has to grip. If it is, as it is with propaganda for carrying through a war, a matter of gathering a whole nation within its circle of influence, there cannot be enough attention paid to avoidance of too high a level of intellectuality. The receptive power of the masses is very limited, their understanding small; on the other hand, they have a great power of forgetting. This being so, all effective propaganda must be confined to a few points.

The Nazi theory of the state, its emphasis on racism, its idolatry of the principle of leadership, its intolerance and one-mindedness, and above all its conception that the individual finds fulfillment through the state, all are consistent in exaggerated form with the traditions of authoritarianism. Nazi Germany could no more resist the imposition of controls on its mass media than it could avoid its "destiny" as the agent for reviving and extending the greatness of the German people.

Thus a common thread runs through all authoritarian theories of governments — from Plato to Hitler. Not all these philosophies were based on the greed for power or for personal aggrandizement. Many were sincere efforts to grapple with the abstruse problems of the nature of the state, the relation of man to the state, and the nature of truth. Regardless of intellectual method or motivation, the result was a system for organizing society under which the mass media were assigned a specific role and were subjected to controls in order not to interfere with the achievement of ultimate ends through the state.

The national states of western Europe were also undoubtedly influenced by the philosophical principles and the tradition of authoritarianism of the Church of Rome. The authority of the church is based on revelation and on its foundation by Christ. It is absolute in so far as it is of divine origin. The immediate center of ecclesiastical authority is the Pope of Rome and the bishops.

Since the church considered itself the depository of revelation entrusted to it by Christ, it felt obliged to preserve this revelation from contamination by any alien influences and to protect the purity of its doctrines from the vacillations and inconsistencies of human opinion. The truth taught by the church was absolute. Therefore it was not subject to deviant secular interpretations. As the shepherd of mankind, the church was responsible for the souls of men, and to fulfill this responsibility it sought to guard its doctrine as well as its adherents from corruption.

The basic principles of the church necessarily led to protective measures in the area of opinion and belief. The church was divinely founded and taught the truth. Other versions of the truth were merely attempts to debase its principles and to seduce its membership from the only path to eternal salvation. Following Platonic precepts, the church provided for the discussion of controversial issues in an area limited to those of the hierarchy. At the same time, it firmly restricted the questioning of fundamental doctrines by those who were not of the hierarchy and who therefore were incompetent to deal with religious doctrine. What the church could do in the spiritual world, a monarchy could do in temporal affairs; and some monarchs, like the British Tudors, thought that they could do both.

This chapter will make no attempt to develop the philosophical bases for the principles of Marxist Communism, although these principles are undoubtedly related to the main stream of authoritarianism. The basic Communist doctrine as it affects the organization and management of the mass media is discussed separately in the final chapter of this volume. Suffice it to say here that Marx, as the saying goes, turned Hegel on his head. Whereas Hegel maintained that the state was the means whereby the individual could achieve self-expression, Marx on the other hand insisted that the relation should be reversed. The individual is not an end in himself but a means to the self-realization of society of which he is an integral part (7:375).

AUTHORITARIAN CONTROL SYSTEMS

Let us now describe and analyze in some detail the operation of the system of mass media control in societies which have to a greater or lesser extent adopted the authoritarian theory. The underlying philosophy of authoritarianism has found expression in many types of governmental organizations, but regardless of the variations, the pattern of control has exhibited a number of common characteristics.

When the authoritarian turns to the functions of the mass media, he has already determined the basic purposes of government. These purposes inevitably control his attitude toward both the cultural and political aspects of communication. Like Plato he arrives through his own logic at a position where it is apparent that the dissemination of information, ideas, and opinions among the members of the community must necessarily have an effect, sometimes immediate and at other times remote, on the accomplishment of predetermined objectives. Often this conclusion is reached through a negative route — by experience with interference by the operators of the channels of communication. Why should those who have access to the mass media, who often are incapable of grasping the totality of purpose of the state, who most often are not completely informed of the objectives of state policy — why should such persons, through their ignorance or stupidity, be permitted to threaten the success of that which has been determined to be for the good of all?

The units of communication should support and advance the policies of the government in power so that this government can achieve its objectives. In the early stages of the development of the mass media, this purpose was usually carried out in its negative aspects through controls which attempted to avoid any interference with the attainment of national ends. In later stages a more positive policy can be discerned. Under it, the state actively participated in the communication process and utilized the mass media as one of the important instruments for accomplishing its purposes.

The first problem under any system of society is to determine who has the right to use the media. Should the avenues of reaching the individual citizen be operated directly by the state; should they be semi-independent instrumentalities subject to surveillance by the state; or should they be open to all who either by past performance or present inclination indicate that they are not likely to interfere with or openly oppose government policies? Authoritarian governments have answered this question in various ways at various times, depending on which policy seemed to provide the greatest chance for success at the moment.

The British Tudors in the sixteenth century answered the problem by granting exclusive patents of monopoly to selected, well-disposed individuals who were permitted to profit from these monopolies so long as they refrained from rocking the ship of state. Elizabeth I found this an inexpensive method of identifying the interests of the printers and publishers of popular literature with the interests of the Crown. Governments in many continental countries of the same period relied on a system of strict surveillance which of course required a bureaucracy to make it effective. Eventually most of the authoritarian governments of the seventeenth and eighteenth centuries, faced with a multiplicity of voices both from within and from without their territories, adopted a policy of actively entering the mass communication field. "Official" journals, representing the government, were established in most western countries. They were charged with giving the populace an "accurate" picture of government activities and with counteracting misconceptions which might be derived from sources which were for one reason or another outside the immediate control of the authorities. However, in contrast with the success in modern Communist countries, no country in western Europe was able for any extended period to monopolize the channels of communication to its people. In most nations, privately and individually operated publications existed alongside the official journals and often provided a competitive service which was superior in most respects.

The major problem in most authoritarian systems was establishing effective restraints and controls over the privately operated media. The western nations tried numerous methods with varying degrees of success, and it can be said that no single method of control was successful over any extended period of time. One of the earliest methods of assuring favorable treatment for government policies was, as has been mentioned, the granting of special "permits" (or "patents," as they were called) to selected individuals to engage in the "art and mystery" of printing. In England this device was expanded in time into an elaborate system of trade regulation. Patents were issued to well-disposed printers for various classes of published works, such as law books, school books, religious books, histories, plays, and many others. Special care went into the selection of printers who were to be entrusted with producing printed matter which concerned affairs of state. When the earliest form of newspaper appeared, it too was assigned to individuals who in return for the exclusive monopoly of purveying news were all too ready to agree to publish only that which forwarded the policies of the state.

In England the patent system flourished for about two hundred years. During that period it apparently was more successful than any other method of control. The British system culminated in an exclusive organization of patentees or "privileged" printers known as the Stationers' Company which through its officers and members was able to police the printing trade at practically no expense to the state. Its royal charter gave the organization power to admit and to expel members from the printing trade and to impose lesser penalties for minor infractions of the trade regulations. The Company was generally assiduous in enforcing its controls since its own monopolistic position depended on its ability to satisfy the government that it was on the side of established authority.

The system of exclusive grants in printing broke down toward the end of the seventeenth century largely because of its own inherent defects and because of the development of private enterprise in all areas of production. In seventeenth-century England the printing monopolists, anxious to expand their production and their profits, trained large numbers of apprentices in the craft. But when the apprentices reached the journeyman stage, they discovered that they could find employment only with a government-licensed publisher. Since government edict limited the number of such publishers and since no new printing enterprises could be established, the distraught journeyman was forced either to accept whatever wages the monopolists offered or to engage in surreptitious publishing as an "outlaw" printer subject to arrest and punishment. In the seventeenth century, printers could readily find both religious and political groups willing to finance the illegal production of tracts and pamphlets which attacked the principles and practices of existing authorities.

The spread of literacy and the consequent demand for more printed materials, the growth of private enterprises in all fields of production, and the spread of religious and political heresies in the form of Protestanism and Democracy — all contributed to the eventual inability of the state to maintain the printing monopolies.

Another closely related technique developed in most countries of western Europe was the licensing system for individual printed works. This system, which in the seventeenth and eighteenth centuries came to be identified with the term "censorship," sometimes operated in conjunction with a licensed or monopolistic press; at other times it kept privately owned printing and publishing establishments under official control. The system was developed under secular auspices in the sixteenth century, when even the monopolistic or state printers were frequently unable or unwilling to follow the lines of government policies. Publishers usually were not privy to state affairs and therefore were unable to make accurate judgments on controversial issues which found their way into print. To remedy this defect, the state required published works in specified areas such as religion and politics to be submitted for examination by its representatives who presumably were acquainted with what the state was attempting to do. In the sixteenth century this was not too difficult a task since the number of published works was relatively small and the duty of examination could be assigned to a secretary of the principal religious and secular authorities.

By the end of the seventeenth century, however, the difficulty of providing an adequate check on the large quantity of materials issued from the press became apparent. The increase in the number and complexity of governmental problems added to the censor's burden. Printers and publishers naturally became irritated with the delays and vacillations inherent in the system and often expressed their dissatisfaction. Even the censors themselves were not happy with a duty which made them responsible for satisfying the varying demands of public policy and public personages. To prejudge the developments of official governmental objectives and strategies as well as the effects of particular published statements became an almost impossible task. It was one which astute politicians on their way to the top assiduously avoided. Better to let an underling make the decisions and take the subsequent criticism.

The system of censoring individual items of printed matter also became increasingly difficult as the newspaper became the principal purveyor of public information. The pressure of weekly and later daily deadlines, the sheer volume of copy, and the cleverness and subtlety of journalistic writers tended to confound the censors. No one of consequence wanted the job, least of all the person who was politically ambitious. In England the system died toward the end of the seventeenth century because of its cumbersomeness and most of all because by then political parties were being formed in the democratic tradition. These parties were unwilling to trust one another with the direction and exclusive control of such an important instrument for achieving and maintaining political power.

In the Anglo-American legal tradition, censorship meant the legal requirement that all materials to be printed and offered for general distribution must first obtain an official permit or license, or, as it was called by the Roman Catholic church, an imprimatur. This type of regulation as practiced under authoritarian philosophies was more common than any other. It was practiced by the governments of France, Germany, Spain, and the Italian states as well as by the early colonial governments in America. In modern times the word censorship has been used in a broader sense, particularly by social scientists, to include all forms of regulation whether they are in the form of licensing or not. The earlier meaning however continues to be used by legal scholars and some historians.

A third general method of press control which authoritarian states employed was prosecution before the courts for violation of accepted or established legal rules of behavior. This method tended to develop later than those previously discussed. It was usually adopted after state monopolies or licensing had failed to accomplish the necessary control. This method also represented an advance in practice since the courts of law generally permitted an individual to take advantage of the legal protections which were available to persons accused of crime. This was particularly true in England, where the courts for many generations had built up a body of procedural law for the protection of the innocent.

Two traditional areas of the law — treason and sedition — were the basis for prosecutions of persons accused or suspected of disseminating information or opinions inimical to the authorities. In any organized society, authoritarian or otherwise, treason is the basic crime against society. In most systems of jurisprudence, it is the keystone of the legal structure which supports the state. Three categories of acts constituted treason. To attempt to overturn the state was treason; to engage in activities which might lead to the overthrow of the established government was also treason; and in many states to advocate policies which might lead to an overthrow was an activity identifiable as treason. Individuals or groups which tried to reach the public through the channels of mass communication could be encompassed by either the second or the third category above. The publisher of a newspaper or leaflet which attacked the government could readily be accused of "activities which might lead to the overthrow of the state."

Another aspect of treason also threatened the printer and publisher in the sixteenth and seventeenth centuries. In most countries of Europe, the state was identified with a particular ruler or monarch. To threaten the position of the monarch was to threaten the stability of the state and was therefore treason. The penalty for treason was usually death, a penalty which in certain periods of history made it a particularly potent weapon against dissent. In other periods with a different climate of opinion, the death penalty was a handicap in obtaining convictions since it did not seem reasonable under some circumstances to apply the extreme penalty to some of the casual and rather innocuous remarks about a regime or a reigning monarch.

In England prosecution for treason was never widely used to punish printers and publishers. Only three printers were executed for publishing material which threatened the security of the state, one in the sixteenth, one in the seventeenth, and one in the eighteenth century. In many modern countries the crime was carefully circumscribed by either constitutional or statutory restrictions to make it unavailable for the prosecution of opinions. In recent years, however, the crime has been revived by both libertarian and authoritarian governments to punish persons who in wartime have tried to assist the enemy and to discourage their homelands through materials broadcast by radio.

Control of the press under authoritarian governments was also facilitated by the development of a branch of the law known as seditious libel or sedition. Treason was reserved for activities which shook the foundations of the state; sedition was used for the irritating flea-bites of the dissident and the nonconformist.

All countries of western Europe during the authoritarian period developed a legal method of bringing before the courts individuals who were attempting by public argument or exhortation to change either the personnel or the practices of the state. Under seventeenth-century theories of monarchy, the ruler was the fountainhead of justice and law, and his acts were beyond popular criticism. "If the ruler is regarded as the superior of the subject, as being by the nature of his position presumably wise and good . . . it must necessarily follow that it is wrong to censure him openly, that even if he is mistaken his mistakes should be pointed out with the utmost respect, and that whether mistaken or not, no censure should be cast upon him likely or designed to diminish his authority" (24:299).

In many states, prosecutions for sedition were conducted without any of the safeguards now associated with criminal trials. In England, however, even the trials for seditious libel, which were so prevalent during the period of the Stuart monarchs, were circumscribed by established judicial procedures common to all forms of criminal prosecutions. These safeguards developed as a reaction against the arbitrary prosecutions for political crimes in the well-publicized proceedings of the English Court of the Star Chamber. Transferred to the common law courts, crimes against the state became less arbitrary in procedure without destroying the effectiveness of the remedy.

A prosecution for seditious libel was the principal weapon against printers and publishers under the authoritarian Stuart monarchs. The Crown stimulated the prosecution, appointed the judges, and provided the witnesses. The law defined the crime which came in time to embrace all types of public criticism and censure. Whatever the authorities disliked was considered a basis for a prosecution for sedition. The doctrine was firmly established by Chief Justice Holt of the Court of King's Bench in his pronouncement:

> This is a very strange doctrine to say that it is not a libel reflecting on the government, endeavouring to possess the people that the government is maladministered by corrupt persons. . . . To say that corrupt officers are appointed to administer affairs is certainly a reflection on the government. If people should not be called to account for possessing the people with an ill opinion of the government, no government can subsist. For it is very necessary for all governments that the people should have a good opinion of it. And nothing can be worse to any government than to endeavour to procure animosities as to the management of it; this has always been looked upon as a crime, and no government can be safe without it (20:1095).

During the eighteenth century, the abandonment of many authoritarian principles in government, the rise of political parties, and the spread of democratic doctrines made it difficult to enforce the law of seditious libel. Although prosecutors continued to arrest and bring to trial persons who criticized the government or its officers, and although judges insisted on defining the law in terms of authoritarian principles, juries revolted and refused to bring in general verdicts of guilty. Experience with juries both in England and in the American colonies forced the authorities to seek other weapons against the constantly increasing activity of the publishers of newspapers and pamphlets.

Throughout the eighteenth century, authoritarianism was on the defensive and libertarian principles were on the march. The traditional weapons against interference with government such as state monopolies, licensing, and prosecutions were becoming less effective. Other means had to be found for protecting the authority of the state. The methods devised were less obvious in their purposes and more devious in their operation. Instead of official journals managed by government appointees, privately owned newspapers were purchased or subsidized with state funds. During Walpole's long regime as first minister in England, political writers were secretly put on the payroll, newspapers were tied to the government through funds from the secret service account, and opposition editors were alternately threatened with prosecution and seduced with bribes. Dictator governments in modern times have tended to continue these practices as an effective method of reducing public criticism and of maintaining a coterie in power.

These indirect methods of control of the media of mass communications have the advantage of allaying attacks from libertarian sources since it is usually difficult, if not impossible, to trace the source of corruption. And even if the fact of control can be established, the authorities can always fall back on the argument that since private interests use the press for their own advantage, the government also is entitled to use whatever means are at hand for creating a favorable attitude toward its officers and policies.

Another indirect method of control which was popular in the eighteenth and nineteenth centuries was a system of special taxes designed to limit both the circulation and the profit in printed matter, especially newspapers seeking a mass audience. A newspaper depending on a mass circulation for its financial success was by that fact less dependent on government subsidies; therefore it tended to become more truculent in its treatment of government affairs. Special taxes on advertising and on circulation tended to reduce the profits of newspapers without making an issue of the editorial contents. The British "taxes on knowledge" became a violent political issue during the first half of the nineteenth century. They were finally abolished by 1861 (22:322).

PERMITTED AND FORBIDDEN SUBJECT MATTER

The principal instruments for controlling the mass media under authoritarian states have been described in broad outlines. Now let us turn to the types of content which were considered to be obnoxious and therefore forbidden. Under the authoritarian philosophy of the nature and function of the state, all instrumentalities operating within the state should advance the objectives and policies of the state. The mass media as an important instrumentality in society fell within this general principle, and their content was tested and evaluated against its contribution to the achievement of established goals. It was not the function of the media either to determine or to question these goals. That function was reserved for the individual or group exercising political power.

The authoritarians did not often object to a discussion of political systems in broad philosophical terms. Unlike the modern Communists, they did not demand complete conformance to a set of theoretical principles. They were usually content if the media avoided direct criticism of current political leaders and their projects, and with a benevolence uncommon in modern Communist and Fascist circles, they tolerated a wide divergence from the political principles upon which their system rested. What was not tolerated was an overt attempt to unseat the authorities themselves. The political machinery might be subject to question; the manipulators of that machinery were not. Elizabeth I in the sixteenth century permitted and sometimes even encouraged a wide latitude of discussion on current issues so long as her authority to make the ultimate decisions was not questioned.

The area of permissible discussion widened as the pyramid of groups within society narrowed. The public at large, the mass of subjects, were considered to be incapable of understanding political problems. Therefore, any discussion by this group was limited. Media attempting to reach this level of society were more carefully watched because of the danger of disturbing the masses or of causing them to develop an interest in that which they were incapable of comprehending and for which they had no direct responsibility. A wider latitude of discussion was permissible in the general assemblies which were frequently a part of authoritarian political machinery. The members of this group were charged with public responsibilities. Thus theoretically they could be trusted to confine their discussions to methods of assisting the central authority to accomplish its objectives. But even in these assemblies there were frequent lapses, and a monarch had occasionally to inform the group that it was transgressing on the powers of the Crown. The most important discussions were reserved for the privy council of advisors who because of their dependence on the central authority could be trusted with "secrets of state."

Information on government affairs, as distinguished from discussion of government policies, followed the same general pattern. In most authoritarian states there was practically no published information on the issues and arguments presented at meetings of the central advisory body. The only decisions announced were those requiring general public compliance or support. Even the general assemblies closely guarded their doors against public curiosity, and members who discussed the proceedings outside the walls of the meeting place were frequently punished. Since the assembly was not representative in the democratic tradition, there was no reason why pressures or instructions from the masses should handicap its deliberations. Here again the theory of public responsibility came into play. Since the assembly was a body with traditional responsibilities, it should be permitted to operate in an atmosphere free from interference by individuals or groups without such responsibilities.

AUTHORITARIANISM AND OTHER THEORIES

As indicated in the preface, this volume discusses four major theories of the role and function of the mass media in society. Before proceeding to discuss some contemporary applications, it might be useful at this point to attempt to point up some of the similarities and some of the differences between the authoritarian theory and the other three. Among the four, the authoritarian and the Marxist-Soviet theories have the greatest number of similarities, while the authoritarian and the libertarian philosophies have the least in common.

Marxist political theories were derived from the early authoritarians and were modified to take into account the industrial revolution and the problems it created. To accomplish its aims Communism teaches the necessity of setting up a dictatorship of the proletariat through the Communist Party. This dictatorship, which in Communist theory may be only a transition stage until the remnants of capitalism are liquidated, conforms in theory to other historical types of absolutism. The media of mass communication owe a duty to support the state. They achieve their own ends by assisting in achieving the ends of the state.

However, the Soviet system differs from other authoritarian systems in two respects. First, the Communists place a greater emphasis on the positive use of the mass media as part of the agitation for the accomplishment of a world revolution. Under Communism the state is not content to restrict the mass media from interfering with state policies; it actively employs the media for the accomplishment of its objectives. A second difference and the most important one is that under Communism the state holds a monopoly over all avenues of reaching the masses. Other dictatorships in the past have allowed the mass media or the major part of them to remain in private hands as private capitalistic enterprises, but under Communism the state "on behalf of the public" owns and operates all units of the mass media. Not only does the state operate the internal media but sets up, in so far as it is able, a complete monopoly of communication by imposing severe restrictions on the importation of foreign-originated materials. This is accomplished by an embargo on the importation of foreign printed media and by a strict control of receiving sets for the electronic media. (For further details on the Soviet methods, see Chapter 4.)

The authoritarian system differs most from the libertarian doctrines of freedom of the press. The entire philosophical basis for a free exchange of ideas is foreign to authoritarian thinking. Since authority rests in the state and since the responsibility for the solution of public issues follows authority, the first duty of the press is to avoid interference with the objectives of the state. These objectives are determined by a ruler or by an elite rather than in "the market place of ideas," as predicated by the libertarians. The idea that the press constitutes a check on government does not make sense to the authoritarian who immediately asks the question — who checks the press?

It should be noted that in modern times many of the national governments which are basically authoritarian in nature have added a number of libertarian trappings to their organizations just as most democratic states today retain vestiges of absolutism, and both authoritarian and libertarian states have in many cases incorporated some of the features of socialism. This is particularly true in the area of the mass media of communication. Hitler recognized the need for keeping his countrymen informed on the essential issues facing his government and permitted selected units of the press to operate on a capitalistic free-enterprise basis. On the other hand, the authoritarians frequently nationalized or socialized many of the media, particularly the more recent units in the electronic field. Radio was always a state monopoly under modern totalitarian governments.

The authoritarian theories have a number of elements in common with the recently developed social responsibility theory of the press (see Chapter 3). Both agree that the press should not be permitted to degrade the culture of a nation, and both postulate that when definite goals for society are determined (by different methods, however) the mass media should not be permitted to interfere irresponsibly with the accomplishment of these objectives. Both systems recognize that there is a relationship between responsibility and action, but they tend to approach the problem from opposite points of view. The authoritarian denies that the press has the responsibility for determining either objectives or the method of achieving them, and because of lack of such responsibility the press should refrain from assuming a duty which is reserved for the central authority. The advocates of the theory of social responsibility, however, retain the democratic tradition that the public ultimately makes decisions, and they charge the press with the duty of informing and guiding the public in an intelligent discussion. The press has the duty to keep the public alert and not to divert its attention or its energies to the irrelevant or the meaningless. The authoritarian and the Communist are convinced that the state must control this process; the libertarian asserts that the less political authority has to do with the process the better; and the advocates of the theory of social responsibility contend that, although libertarian principles may be basically sound, their operation in the complex of contemporary society demands some form of control, preferably by the media themselves with a benevolent government in the background unobtrusively checking the ground rules.

AUTHORITARIANISM IN THE MODERN WORLD

We now turn to some contemporary manifestations of the operation of the authoritarian concept of the status and function of the mass media in society. We shall make no attempt to describe the status of the press in the pre-World War II regimes of Hitler and Mussolini since both are largely of historical interest today.[1]

There can be no question but that in the world at large, outside the Russian Soviet orbit, the authoritarian theorists have had to admit the

---

[1] For a compilation of the laws of the rigidly controlled Italian press of the Mussolini era, in which the writer emphasizes the "singular imprint and high political mission" given the press by Fascism, see 13.

The conversion of the German press into an instrument for government propaganda has been described in 12. The state of the German press, publishing, radio and cinema is described in greater detail in a book-length study of German propaganda, 23.

ascendency of libertarian principles. Nevertheless, the libertarian doctrines are frequently merely window dressing behind which governments follow authoritarian practices. United Nations surveys in which national governments report on the situation in their countries indicate that belief in freedom of expression is so strong a popular conviction everywhere that all countries possessing information media claim to have a free press. However, freedom of expression in many nations has been shaped to fit a pattern that has very little in common with the western democratic concept.

The conflict between democratic principles and authoritarian practices in the world today is described in a report prepared by Salvador P. Lopez at the request of the Economic and Social Council of the United Nations from which the following is quoted:

In a world racked by ideological contention and insurgent nationalism, there has grown an ever-sharpening struggle for the minds of men. Highly developed techniques are being employed for the purpose of information, propaganda and indoctrination with the result that each is often indistinguishable from the others.

Inevitably in this struggle, the basic human right to freedom of opinion and expression has become, in many parts of the world, a casualty. This is true in the authoritarian States, but even in other countries this right is constantly menaced by the tendency to sacrifice freedom in the ostensible interest of defending freedom. The result is a complex social and political problem, marked by continuous interplay between abuse and efforts to correct abuses, between attempts to restrict freedom and attempts to widen it (14:15).

The same report contains an appendix prepared by the secretariat of the International Press Institute (Zurich) which attempts to assess the extent of libertarian and authoritarian practices in the world today:

The majority of the 248 editors in 41 countries who answered the questionnaire added that there was a growing tendency, in democratic as well as in non-democratic countries, to restrict the free gathering of the legitimate news (14:60).

.   .   .   .

Freedom of information is being especially threatened today. The experience of governments during the Second World War when the press had to accept severe curtailment of its liberty, and the special requirements of security in the succeeding "cold war" account partly for the tendency towards Press restriction. The fact that some countries are still technically at war helps to justify controls not only for themselves but in neighboring countries. Further, in some cases, quarrels between neighbors, of whom one is totalitarian and the other democratic, lead to efforts to limit the freedom of opinion expressed in the latter (14:61).

The Zurich report sets up the following categories:

1. Countries where press control is complete. Examples: Soviet Union and its satellites, China, Yugoslavia, Portugal, Spain.

2. Countries where political criticism by the press is formally possible but where censorship operates. Examples: Colombia, Egypt, Syria.

3. Countries where special press laws or other discriminatory legislation expose editors to arrest and persecution. Examples: Union of South Africa, Iran, Pakistan, India, Iraq, Lebanon.

4. Countries where unofficial methods discourage press opposition. Examples: Turkey, Argentina, Indonesia.[2]

At a meeting of the International Press Institute in Copenhagen in May, 1955, it was reported that in the last few years more than one hundred newspapers including the internationally known *La Prensa* have been silenced in Argentina. Many of these journals were closed on such charges as publishing a photograph showing crowds in demonstration, selling rationed newsprint illegally, and the lack of hygienic facilities in the plant (27:74).

Another attempt to survey press practices on a regional basis is made periodically by the Freedom of the Press Committee of the Inter-American Press Association. The report covering the period October, 1954, to April, 1955, stated: "Six months ago it was reported that approximately 20% of the inhabitants of the Western hemisphere live under one or another form of censorship. There has been little improvement since then with the sole exception of Nicaragua. Freedom of the press does not exist or is limited in one way or another in Argentina, Bolivia, Colombia, Dominican Republic, Paraguay, Peru and Venezuela" (2:12).

The American news service, the Associated Press, has for several years made a semiannual survey of world press conditions gathered by its correspondents. The survey for the last six months of 1954 reported little change in the status of the press from that reported in previous surveys. Authoritarian practices were found in some Latin American countries and in the Middle East. Domestic publications

---

[2] It should be pointed out that the above examples were listed on the basis of data received in 1953. The status of the press in some of the countries listed may have since changed.

were reported to be under strict control in Portugal, Spain, Yugoslavia, Iran, Egypt, Iraq, and Saudi Arabia. Communist China maintains complete internal control of all media. Publishers have been arrested in Peru; newspapers expropriated in Colombia; reports censored in Venezuela. After several years of expropriation by the Peron government, the famous Argentine newspaper, *La Prensa*, was restored to its owners. In Brazil censorship of domestic newspapers was imposed after the political upheaval in November, 1955 (18:4).

The New York *Times* commented editorially from a libertarian point of view on the survey for the first six months of 1954 as follows:

Many Governments still do not dare allow their own people or the world at large to know what is going on in the territories they control. This is the gist of the latest Associated Press report on censorship made public yesterday. The whole truth is not available in Russia, China or any Communist controlled country; nor in Yugoslavia, which has its own anti-Moscow brand of Communism; nor in other dictator-ruled countries such as Spain, Portugal, and Argentina; nor in Bolivia, Venezuela, Saudi Arabia, Iran, and Egypt. . . . The reasons for censorship do not change. Censorship is always and everywhere intended to conceal facts that might hurt those in power (17:10).

As indicated previously, most nations of the world outside the Communist orbit tend under the pressure of world opinion to give at least lip service to the principles of libertarianism in their official pronouncements on the status of the mass media. One of the few countries which unequivocally states its authoritarian position is Portugal. The constitution of Portugal (Article 22) contains the following provision: "Public opinion is a fundamental element of the politics and administration of the country; it shall be the duty of the state to protect it against all those agencies which distort it contrary to truth, justice, good administration and the common welfare." The constitution of Portugal also provides (Article 23) that since the press exercises a public function it may not therefore refuse to insert any official notices of normal dimensions on matters of national importance sent to it by the government.

A point of view somewhat similar to that of Portugal is expressed in a provision of the constitution of Ecuador (Article 187) which asserts that "the primary aim of journalism is to defend the national interests, and it constitutes a social service worthy of the respect and support of the state."

The Egyptian authorities have also been forthright in their public announcement of their policy toward the press. The following is quoted from a proclamation issued on January 26, 1952:

In the interests of national security, a general censorship is hereby established and shall continue to operate until further notice throughout the territory and territorial waters of Egypt. The censorship shall be applied to all written or printed matter, photographs, packets and parcels entering or leaving or circulating in Egypt; all messages sent by telegraphy or telephony, whether wireless or otherwise; all news, information or other broadcast matter; theatrical performances, cinematography films, phonograph records or any other means of aural or visual reproduction, provided that all matter and all messages originated by or addressed to the Royal Egyptian Government shall be exempt from censorship control (26:55-56).

Although both India and Pakistan have adopted constitutional provisions for protecting liberty of expression in the western libertarian tradition, both countries have found it difficult to avoid authoritarian practices. They generally justify these practices on the basis of national security. The Supreme Court of India has ruled that the constitutional guarantee of freedom of expression permits legislation requiring the deposit of a security bond from a publisher accused of circulating objectionable matter. (*State of Bihar* vs. *Shailabala Devi,* Supreme Court of India, May 26, 1952, set out in 26:131-32.) In Pakistan an act was passed in 1952 "to provide for special measures to deal with persons acting in a manner prejudicial to the defense, external affairs and security of Pakistan." The act permits the central government to expel any foreigner or to impose such restrictions on nationals as may be specified in the order. Among the powers granted in the act is one requiring that "all matter or any matter relating to a particular subject shall before being published be submitted for scrutiny to an authority specified in the order." The central government is also empowered to "prohibit for a specified period the publication of any newspaper, periodical, leaflet or other publication." (Act No. XXV of 1952, quoted in full in 26:212-16.)

A not uncommon practice in some countries professing libertarian principles is the suspending of all constitutional protection for civil rights for a specified period. For example, the Legislative Assembly of El Salvador in a decree of September 26, 1952, suspended for thirty days the safeguards of Articles 154, 158 (1), 159, and 160 of the constitution which included freedom of expression and dissemination of opinion, secrecy of correspondence, and freedom of association and assembly.

The development of the motion picture as a medium of entertainment and information has posed some special problems of regulation and control for both the authoritarian and libertarian states. For countries operating on authoritarian principles, the problem was merely to develop machinery and techniques for accomplishing predetermined objectives. In libertarian countries, the movies presented a host of new issues which even today have not been completely solved. (See Chapter 2, p. 62.)

In practically all countries of the world, the theater has been subjected to official supervision in one form or another. The early motion picture was so closely associated with the theater both in function (entertainment) and presentation (in theaters) that governments commonly applied the same philosophy and the same regulations to both forms of presentation. However, several differences soon appeared, among them the development of educational films, documentaries, and newsreels; the rise of giant monopolistic film-producing centers, particularly in the United States; and above all the enhanced effects of the motion picture on an enlarged and frequently poorly educated audience.

Under authoritarian principles, the basic problem was not too complex. The motion picture should be treated exactly like other media of mass communication. Like books, magazines, and newspapers, the film should not interfere with the attainment of the objectives of the state; if at all possible, it should definitely contribute to the attainment of those goals. The only question was how best to accomplish these purposes. Some governments set up an official unit within one of the ministries, charged with supervising and censoring motion pictures. Recent information on the methods employed in various foreign states is difficult to find, but in many countries the official supervisory body is attached to the Department of Education or is a separate group composed of members from various divisions of the government.[3]

That the motion picture, whether a feature film, a documentary or a newsreel, can have a powerful effect on public attitudes and opinions is unquestioned. Both Nazi Germany and Fascist Italy placed strict embargoes on American films just prior to World War II on the ground that they were propaganda for the libertarian concept and

---

[3] A compilation of methods of regulation employed by foreign governments was made by John E. Harley in 1940 and published as Chapter V of *World-Wide Influences of the Cinema*, Los Angeles, University of Southern California Press, 1940.

for American policy. Hitler, like the Soviet-Russians, took the position that all art forms should conform to the ideals of the state and should not in any way detract from or debase these ideals. The situation is described by John E. Harley, chairman of the Committee on International Relations of the American Institute of Cinematography, as follows:

It is a matter of common observation that American films have largely molded the views and ideas of peoples throughout the world as regards the United States and its people. This point may be accepted as well founded. The extreme care exercised by national censors shows how keenly they appreciate the power of the cinema over their people. No thoughtful person can study the rules of censorship of the various nations without being struck by the national censorial solicitude for the cultural screen diet imported from abroad or made at home. Many persons will doubtless smile when they compare the rules of censorship as they exist in various countries (8:2).

Because of the political and cultural influence of the film, many countries including democracies have attempted to expand national film production and distribution through both financial aid and protective measures. Hollywood's dominance of the world film market has tended to accelerate these efforts. Great Britain, France, Italy, and Argentina are examples of countries which subsidize the film industry as a matter of public policy (19:167-77).

Authoritarian governments gave equally definite answers to the problem of controlling and regulating the newer electronic media of mass communication, radio and television broadcasting. Two factors dictated state policy on these media. First, the general principles of authoritarianism provided a solid basis for regulation. Radio and television, like the older media, must further the interests of government and must help to advance the cultural and political objectives of the central authority. The second factor was the nature of the media as electronic communication. All types of broadcasting required the use of electromagnetic waves, of which the supply was limited. These channels were the property of the state; consequently their use was subject to state control.

Most authoritarian states have established complete state monopolies of broadcasting. The operation and programming of both radio and television rest with an official government agency which is responsible for carrying out government objectives. Practically no authoritarian state has adopted the British system of a public corporation or the American system of privately owned free-enterprise broadcasting.

Since broadcasting of all kinds does not limit its signal to the territorial boundaries of a national state, several special problems of control and regulation arise. First, which country gets what part of the electronic spectrum? This question has presented international complications and has resulted in several world conferences on frequency assignments. In most of the world, the internal national use of the air waves is controlled by international agreements which were negotiated under the auspices of the International Telecommunications Union. The assignment of specific channels to national governments is subject to international negotiation and in large part has been settled on by general agreement. An exception is the use of short-wave frequencies for international broadcasting, which is still an issue on which the major countries have been unable to agree.

A second problem inherent in the nature of broadcasting is the internal control of signals emanating from outside the national borders of a state. Books, magazines, newspapers, and films can be stopped at the border and inspected for objectionable content. Radio messages, because they ignore national borders, present an irritating problem to many governments. One solution is to ignore international agreements and to "jam" the wave lengths of neighboring states. Another is to establish rigid controls over the possession and use of receiving sets.

SUMMARY

The modern theory of authoritarianism is aptly summed up by the well-known British writer, Dr. Samuel Johnson, who took part in the eighteenth-century controversy over the values of authority and liberty:

Every society has a right to preserve public peace and order, and therefore has a good right to prohibit the propagation of opinions which have a dangerous tendency. To say the magistrate has this right is using an inadequate word; it is the society for which the magistrate is agent. He may be morally or theologically wrong in restraining the propagation of opinions which he thinks dangerous, but he is politically right . . . (1:249).

The danger of . . . unbounded liberty and the danger of bounding it have produced a problem in the science of government, which human understanding seems hitherto unable to solve. If nothing may be published but what civil authority shall have previously approved, power must always be the standard of truth; if every dreamer of innovations may propagate his projects, there can be no settlement; if every murmur at government may diffuse discontent, there can be no peace; and if every skeptic in theology may teach his follies, there can be no religion (11:107-08).

As was stated at the opening of this chapter, large segments of the globe over extended periods have accepted the basic principles of authoritarianism as a guide for social action. These principles have been particularly pervasive in the control, regulation, and utilization of the media of mass communication. And although the theories themselves have been discarded in most democratic countries, the practices of authoritarian states have tended to influence democratic practices. In some instances they have almost forced libertarian governments to take countersteps which in some aspects are indistinguishable from the totalitarian models.

THE LIBERTARIAN

THEORY OF

THE PRESS

FRED S. SIEBERT 2

Like other theories of the status and function of the mass media of communication in society, the libertarian doctrine is a development of the philosophical principles which provide the basis for the social and political structure within which the media operate. Liberalism, as a social and political system, has a set framework for the institutions which function within its orbit, and the press, like other institutions, is conditioned by the principles underlying the society of which it is a part.

For the last century, a large part of the civilized world has professed to adhere to the principles of liberalism. Today, except for the countries under Communist domination, most nations at least theoretically have based their social and political organizations on the theories of liberalism. With such a wide cultural and geographical dispersal of these doctrines, it is not surprising that there should have developed significant variations in the practical workings of social institutions, including the mass media of communication. For instance, broadcasting as it operates in the United States may have very little in common with broadcasting under a libertarian government such as France or Brazil.

BASIC POSTULATES

To understand the principles governing the press under democratic governments, one must understand the basic philosophy of liberalism as it developed in the seventeenth and eighteenth centuries. The democratic nations of today owe their birth to principles which gradually evolved from the theoretical explorations of a large number of individual thinkers. Those thinkers in turn were directly influenced in their speculations by the social, political, and economic events of their times.

The principles of libertarian philosophy, as of authoritarianism, are based on the answers to questions about the nature of man, the nature of society and man's relation to it, and the nature of knowledge and of truth. Although libertarian philosophers may differ widely, they have a number of common bonds which identify them as belonging to a general school or system of philosophy.

Man, say the libertarians, is a rational animal and is an end in himself. The happiness and well-being of the individual is the goal of society, and man as a thinking organism is capable of organizing the world around him and of making decisions which will advance his interests. Although men frequently do not exercise their God-given powers of reason in solving human problems, in the long run they tend, by the aggregate of their individual decisions, to advance the cause of civilization. Man differs from lower animals in his ability to think, to remember, to utilize his experience, and to arrive at conclusions. Because of this unique ability, man is unique. He is the prime unit of civilization as well as its mover. The fulfillment of the individual therefore becomes the ultimate goal — the goal of man, of society, and of the state.

Libertarians have given varying accounts of the origin of society, but all agree that the prime function of society is to advance the interests of its individual members. Many adherents of liberalism cast a nostalgic eye at man in a state of nature where he was unencumbered by much of the paraphernalia of civilization. Although society undoubtedly can contribute much to the well-being of man, at the same time protections should be found against the tendency of society to take over the major role and become an end in itself. The philosophers of liberalism emphatically deny that the state is the highest expression of human endeavor, although they admit with some hesitancy that the state is a useful and even necessary instrument. The state exists as a method of providing the individual with a milieu in which he can realize his own potentialities. When it fails to further this end, it becomes a handicap which should be either abolished or drastically modified. Liberal philosophy does not accept the proposition that a society becomes a separate entity of greater importance than the individual members which comprise it.

The libertarian theory of the nature of knowledge and of truth strongly resembles the theological doctrines of early Christianity. The power to reason was God-given just as the knowledge of good and evil was God-given. With such an inheritance from his Maker, man could achieve an awareness of the world around him through his own efforts. On this foundation, the libertarians built a superstructure which differed drastically from that developed by the philosophers of the Middle Ages. Man's inheritance became less important and his individual ability to solve the problems of the universe more obvious. Reason was to act upon the evidence of the senses, not as in earlier times after all authority had been exhausted, but as the only way to find an authoritative explanation. Truth was something which might be different from what had previously been taught (as the Reformation contended), but it was still a definite discoverable entity capable of demonstration to all thinking men. The conception that there is one basic unassailable and demonstrable explanation for natural phenomena as developed by mechanistic experimentation and observation became the model upon which libertarian philosophers proceeded to generalize in all areas of knowledge. Although the path to truth might lie through a morass of argument and dispute, that which lay at the end of the path was definite, provable, and acceptable to rational men.

THE DEVELOPMENT OF LIBERALISM

The sixteenth century provided the experiences; the seventeenth century saw the development of the philosophical principles; and the eighteenth century put these principles into practice. Harold Laski, whose *The Rise of European Liberalism* is the foremost history and analysis of western liberalism, has pointed out that social philosophy is always the offspring of history and is unintelligible save in terms of the events from which it arose. The geographical discoveries of the sixteenth century provided a new spaciousness for the minds of men. They were directly responsible for the expansion and consequent protection of trade and for the destruction of traditional attitudes through knowledge of foreign peoples and foreign customs.

Scientific as well as geographical discoveries influenced the minds of men by emphasizing the rationality of the universe and the possibility of understanding it through patient analysis. The seventeenth century was convinced that everything in the universe was controlled by a set of laws which could be reduced to a strict mathematical formulation. Newton, Copernicus, Kepler, and Tycho Brahe laid the basis for the construction of a new mechanistic universe. Progress in the western sense took on a new significance. This was a new age with new ways of thinking. Descartes was probably the principal figure in the shift from the old to the new. By insisting on the supremacy of reason, he challenged the whole faith of power and authority. Implicit in his philosophy was the supremacy of a secular as opposed to a theological conception of the universe. Man was forced to rely on himself rather than on a divine Providence.

Although the Reformation was both a theological and political dispute, it became the reluctant parent of western liberalism. The Puritans in England, with the Bible as their authority, revolted against the authority of the church, but they soon discovered that they were encouraging the habit of individual judgment. And rationalism in religion inevitably led to sectarianism, to deism, and to secularism. The Reformation also produced a pattern of discussion and argument which was congenial to the times, and because religion and politics were so interwoven, this pattern was readily transferred to the purely secular arena.

Another factor affecting the development of liberalism was the emergence of the middle class. In most countries of western Europe, the interests of the developing commercial class demanded an end to religious disputes. It also required limitations on monarchial powers and on the special privileges of the nobility. Capitalistic enterprise was incompatible with medieval notions of status and security. The free contract became the basis of the economic liberalism which the age of expansion demanded. Neither the church nor the state was allowed to question the moral adequacy of an acquisitive society which was busily engaged in supplying the wants of men.

England was the principal source of political philosophy in the seventeenth century, a century which began with the complete ascendency of authoritarian principles and which ended with the triumph of liberalism. The Revolution of 1688 resulted in the supremacy of Parliament over the Crown, in the creation of a party system, and above all in the justification of the right of revolution. John Locke was the apologist and theorist for the British developments, and his political philosophy profoundly affected all subsequent western libertarians. Basing his conclusions on empirical methods, Locke developed a theory of popular sovereignty, with the center of power in the will of the people. The government was merely the trustee to which the people had delegated authority and from which they could withdraw it. His political philosophy justified limitations on sovereign power, the existence of popular rights in the form of law, the toleration of a diversity of religious opinions compatible with political unity, and an economic order providing for freedom of individual enterprise. The law of nature and the social compact are essential doctrines of Locke's philosophy. He argued that man under the guise of reason has surrendered his personal rights to the state in return for a guarantee that the state will recognize and maintain his natural rights. He denied the political validity of church government and argued cogently for religious toleration, excluding, of course, elements subversive of the state. The revolutionary aspects of Locke made him a source of inspiration for both the American and French revolutions, and much of his phraseology found its way into the American Declaration of Independence and the French Rights of Man.

The "Enlightenment" of the seventeenth and eighteenth centuries contributed immeasurably toward the acceptance and diffusion of libertarian principles. Its basic aim was to free man from all outside restrictions on his capacity to use his reason for solving religious, political and social problems. "The basic idea underlying all tendencies of enlightenment was the conviction that human understanding is capable, by its own power and without recourse to supernatural assistance, of comprehending the system of the world and that this new way of understanding the world will lead to a new way of mastering it. Enlightenment sought to gain universal recognition for this principle in the natural and intellectual sciences, in physics, and ethics, in the philosophies of religion, history, law, and politics" (37:547).

LIBERALISM AND THE PRESS

With this background, we can now discuss the effects of libertarian philosophy on the status and function of the mass media of communication. The important contributions of liberalism in this area were the insistence on the importance of the individual, the reliance on his powers of reasoning, and the concept of natural rights, of which freedom of religion, speech and press became a part. The late Professor Carl Becker has stated the basic assumptions succinctly:

The democratic doctrine of freedom of speech and of the press, whether we regard it as a natural and inalienable right or not, rests upon certain assumptions. One of these is that men desire to know the truth and will be disposed to be guided by it. Another is that the sole method of arriving at the truth in the long run is by the free competition of opinion in the open market. Another is that, since men will invariably differ in their opinions, each man must be permitted to urge, freely and even strenuously, his own opinion, provided he accords to others the same right. And the final assumption is that from this mutual toleration and comparison of diverse opinions the one that seems the most rational will emerge and be generally accepted (31:33).

The eighteenth century completed the transfer of the press from authoritarian to libertarian principles. At the opening of the century, the authoritarian system of press control was dying. The power of the Crown to regulate the press had been abandoned, the church had been removed as a regulatory agency, and state monopolies in publishing had been abolished. By the end of the century, libertarian principles were enshrined in the fundamental law of the land in constitutional phrases protecting freedom of speech and of the press. At least three Englishmen and one American made significant contributions toward this transition: John Milton in the seventeenth century; John Erskine and Thomas Jefferson in the eighteenth; and John Stuart Mill in the nineteenth.

John Milton, in the *Areopagitica*, published in 1644, wrote a majestic argument for intellectual freedom in the libertarian tradition. Although it is not a comprehensive statement of the principles of freedom of speech and of the press, it was for its time a powerful argument against authoritarian controls. Milton was personally irritated by the Puritan censorship of his own writings and indicted the theory and practice of licensing. Basic to his argument were the assumptions that men by exercising reason can distinguish between right and wrong, good and bad, and that to exercise this talent man should have unlimited access to the ideas and thoughts of other men. Milton was confident that Truth was definite and demonstrable and that it had unique powers of survival when permitted to assert itself in a "free and open encounter." Out of Milton have developed the contemporary concepts of "the open market place of ideas" and the "self-righting process": Let all with something to say be free to express themselves. The true and sound will survive; the false and unsound will be vanquished. Government should keep out of the battle and not weigh the odds in favor of one side or the other. And even though the false may gain a temporary victory, that which is true, by drawing to its defense additional forces, will through the self-righting process ultimately survive.

Milton recognized that the right of free discussion might be limited but he avoided any general principles on which these limitations might be based. He wanted freedom from government censorship for serious-minded men who held honest, although differing, opinions. Because he thought they did not live up to his standards of honesty, he would deny full freedom to Roman Catholics and to the ephemeral journalists of his day. His powerful appeal for intellectual freedom unfortunately had little effect on his contemporaries, but his work was revived in the eighteenth century and widely circulated in England and America.

No comprehensive statement of the problem of the relation of government to the press appeared in print between Milton and John Stuart Mill. Nevertheless the pressure of practical problems of regulation produced a number of additions to, and elaborations of, the Miltonian thesis. Such varying personalities as Lord Camden, John Wilkes, "Junius," and Thomas Paine contributed to both the theory and the application of the concept "freedom of the press." The most articulate of the eighteenth-century group in England was John Erskine. In his defense of publishers accused of violating the law, he advanced the libertarian principles of freedom of speech and press. Erskine made his position clear in defending Paine for publishing *The Rights of Man:* "The proposition which I mean to maintain as the basis of liberty of the press, and without which it is an empty sound, is this: that every man, not intending to mislead, but seeking to enlighten others with what his own reason and conscience, however erroneously, have dictated to him as truth, may address himself to the universal reason of the whole nation, either upon subjects of government in general, or upon that of our own particular country" (46:414).

John Stuart Mill approached the problem of authority versus liberty from the viewpoint of a nineteenth-century utilitarian. For Mill, liberty was the right of the mature individual to think and act as he pleases so long as he harms no one else by doing so. All human action, said Mill, should aim at creating, maintaining, and increasing the greatest happiness for the greatest number of persons; for the good society is one in which the greatest possible number of persons enjoy the greatest possible amount of happiness. One of the main ways for society to insure that its members will contribute most to this end is by giving them the right to think and act for themselves.

Translating these general ideas on liberty to the specific liberty of expression, Mill presents four basic propositions. First, if we silence an opinion, for all we know, we are silencing truth. Secondly, a wrong opinion may contain a grain of truth necessary for finding the whole truth. Third, even if the commonly accepted opinion is the whole truth, the public tends to hold it not on rational grounds but as a prejudice unless it is forced to defend it. Last, unless the commonly held opinion is contested from time to time, it loses its vitality and its effect on conduct and character.

Mill's emphasis on the importance of the individual's freedom of expression is expressed in the following well-known quotation from his work *On Liberty:*

If all mankind minus one, were of one opinion, and only one person were of the contrary opinion, mankind would be no more justified in silencing that one person, than he, if he had the power, would be justified in silencing mankind. Were an opinion a personal possession of no value except to the owner; if to be obstructed in the enjoyment of it were simply a private injury, it would make some difference whether the injury was inflicted on a few persons or on many. But the peculiar evil of silencing the expression of an opinion is, that it is robbing the human race; posterity as well as the existing generation; those who dissent from the opinion, still more than those who hold it. If the opinion is right, they are deprived of the opportunity of exchanging error for truth; if wrong, they lose, what is almost as great a benefit, the clearer perception and livelier impression of truth, produced by its collision with error (52:16).

Thomas Jefferson was both a philosopher and a statesman, a man of ideas and a man of action, who attempted to put his ideas into practice. By fusing the two streams of liberalism, the legalism and traditionalism of England with the more radical rationalism of France, he hoped to create a government which would provide both security and opportunity for the individual. Jefferson was firmly convinced that, although individual citizens may err in exercising their reason, the majority as a group would inevitably make sound decisions. To facilitate this process, the individuals in a society should be educated and informed; hence Jefferson's interest in the instruments of education. For the mature individual, the press was an essential source of information and guidance, and in order properly to perform its function in a democracy, the press should be free from control by the state. Jefferson concluded that the principal function of government was to establish and maintain a framework within which the individual could pursue his own ends. The function of the press was to participate in the education of the individual and at the same time to guard against deviations by government from its original purposes.

Although Jefferson as a political figure suffered greatly from the calumnies of the press of his time, he held to his conviction that, despite its errors and vituperation, the press should be subject to a minimum of interference by the federal government. In his Second Inaugural Address, he even proclaimed that a government which could not stand up under criticism deserved to fall and that the real strength of the federal government was its willingness to permit and its ability to withstand public criticism. Jefferson's conception of the function of the press is summarized in the following:

No experiment can be more interesting than that we are now trying, and which we trust will end in establishing the fact, that man may be governed by reason and truth. Our first object should therefore be, to leave open to him all the avenues to truth. The most effectual hitherto found, is the freedom of the press. It is therefore the first shut up by those who fear the investigation of their actions. The firmness with which the people have withstood the late abuses of the press, the discernment they have manifested between truth and falsehood, show that they may safely be trusted to hear everything true and false, and to form a correct judgment between them. I hold it, therefore, to be certain, that to open the doors of truth, and to fortify the habit of testing everything by reason, are the most effectual manacles we can rivet on the hands of our successors to prevent their manacling the people with their own consent (48:32-34).

The transfer of the mass media from authoritarian to libertarian principles in England and America was not accomplished overnight but over several centuries. The English Bill of Rights of 1689 made no mention of the press. However, press freedom was implicit in the recognition of the insistent demand for the protection of the individual from arbitrary power. The main battle to establish freedom for the mass media was fought in the eighteenth century, and in the vanguard of that fight were the printers and publishers of newspapers. With the abolition of the licensing system in 1694, the press found itself subjected to prosecutions for sedition as well as to more indirect restrictions, such as special taxation, subsidization, and regulations against access to proceedings of Parliament. One by one these obstructions were demolished but not without extended arguments and, on occasions, violent opposition by government officials and their supporters.

There were two main struggles in the eighteenth century to establish libertarian principles as they affected the press. One was concerned with seditious libel; the other dealt with the right of the press to publish the proceedings of government. As was pointed out in Chapter 1, p. 23, the government both in England and in the American colonies sought to control open criticism of its activities by prosecutions for seditious libel. The judges, appointed by the Crown, were often sympathetic with the government's attempt to restrain the press from disturbing the public. During the eighteenth century, the courts adhered to the principle that published material attacking government policies or personnel tended to undermine the state and therefore was illegal. Under the English system of jurisprudence, the question of whether or not the published words were dangerous or "seditious" was obvious from a mere reading of them and therefore could be determined by the judge. The question of whether or not the words were published by the individual brought before the bar was one of fact which could be determined by a jury. Early in the eighteenth century, juries in England and America began to rebel against this division of function. Goaded by both publishers and libertarian political leaders, they refused to bring in convictions. Fox's Libel Act settled the dispute in 1792 by giving the jury the right to determine the harmful tendency of the published material.

A related problem and one which raised more serious questions was whether or not the publisher could justify publishing admittedly harmful words on the ground that they constituted a true and accurate account. Throughout the eighteenth century, jurists contended that words which injured the government were punishable whether true or false. Libertarian principles finally triumphed with the establishment of truth as a defense in America by constitutional provisions and in England by a Parliamentary Act (1843).

Another arena in which libertarian principles battled for ascendency was Parliament, which for centuries had excluded strangers and had prohibited written notes for fear that the public might intrude on the discussions. Toward the end of the eighteenth century, a final skirmish resulted in a triumph for democracy. The newspapers of the time contended that since Parliament represented the interests of the people its debates should be open to the public. The press as a medium for reaching the public therefore had a right as well as a duty to inform the public of what took place in Parliament; consequently Parliament had no right to place restrictions on the exercise of this function. Traditional British officialdom rose up in horror at this contention, but in a series of skirmishes the press emerged the winner.

The contest for recognition of libertarian doctrines as they affected the press culminated in the formulization and adoption of Bills of Rights which included provisions establishing press freedom. This freedom was coupled in many statements with freedom of speech and of religion. Statements on freedom of the press in the early American Bills of Rights preceded provisions on both speech and religion, and in most early discussions were less controversial than the question of religion. In a period covering not more than twenty years, protections for freedom of the press were incorporated into most of the American state constitutions and into the federal constitution.

The wording in the Bills of Rights of the right to freedom of the press was necessarily vague and subject to varying interpretations. On only one point were all interpretations agreed — that freedom of the press was not absolute but was subject to limitations. The problem of what limitations could properly be imposed on the press became the major issue under liberalism.

Eighteenth-century English jurists made the first attempt to define the limits of freedom of the press. Two eminent English judges, Lord Mansfield and Chief Justice Blackstone, advanced an interpretation based on conservative British tradition. Both asserted the superiority of law as defined by the courts and Parliament over the concept of freedom of the press. Both considered censorship in the form of licensing to be illegal. Beyond that they refused to go, contending that control of the abuses of the press was a proper function of law.

Blackstone's statement, widely circulated in the American states, summarizes the eighteenth-century legalistic position:

The liberty of the press is indeed essential to the nature of a free state, but this consists in laying no previous restraints upon publications, and not in freedom from censure for criminal matter when published. Every free man has an undoubted right to lay what sentiments he pleases before the public; to forbid this, is to destroy the freedom of the press; but if he publishes what is improper, mischievous, or illegal, he must take the consequences of his own temerity . . . thus the will of individuals is still left free; the abuse only of that free-will is the object of legal punishment. Neither is any restraint hereby laid upon freedom of thought or inquiry; liberty of private sentiment is still left; the disseminating, or making public, of bad sentiments, destructive of the ends of society, is the crime which society corrects (34:1326-27).

Both Erskine and Jefferson contended for a broader interpretation of the constitutional protection of the press from government control than either Mansfield or Blackstone was willing to accept. The Erskine thesis was that even though the matter published was erroneous and even though it might adversely affect the interests of the state, no penalties should be placed on the publisher who was honest and sincere in his purposes and intent. Jefferson argued that while the press should be subject to punishment for damages to individuals it should not be held liable for injuries to the reputation of the government. Defining the proper limitations on the freedom of the media is the most disturbing problem facing the supporter of libertarian principles. Even today, as we shall see later in this chapter, no agreement has been reached in democratic circles on the proper sphere of government control and regulation of the various types of mass media.

STATUS AND FUNCTION OF THE MASS MEDIA IN DEMOCRATIC SOCIETIES

With that background to help us understand libertarian concepts, we can now examine the status and function of the mass media of communication in democratic societies. In societies based on libertarian principles the status of the press becomes a problem of adjustment to democratic political institutions and to the democratic way of life. Government in a democracy is the servant of the people. As such it occupies a much different relationship to its adherents than does the authoritarian government. Yet even though the government is subservient to and responsible to the public at large, it is not thoroughly trusted to identify its ends with the ends of its citizens. Innumerable devices have been invented in democratic countries to keep governments from reverting to authoritarian practices as well as from subverting the "unalienable rights" of its individual citizens.

The basis for a libertarian press system was developed by Milton and Locke in the seventeenth century, as already described; the details were worked out and put into practice in the eighteenth century; and the system spread throughout the world when liberalism was at its zenith, in the nineteenth century. Practically all democratic countries in the world adopted the libertarian theories and embodied them in their constitutions or fundamental laws.

Under the libertarian concept, the functions of the mass media of communication are to inform and to entertain. A third function was developed as a necessary correlate to the others to provide a basis of economic support and thus to assure financial independence. This was the sales or advertising function. Basically the underlying purpose of the media was to help discover truth, to assist in the process of solving political and social problems by presenting all manner of evidence and opinion as the basis for decisions. The essential characteristic of this process was its freedom from government controls or domination. The government together with its officials was frequently a party with a direct interest in the outcome of a dispute. Therefore, it should not have the additional advantage of exclusive access to the public which ultimately made the decisions. Neither should it have the right or the power to interfere with the presentation of arguments from the opposition. Thus there developed a refinement of the function of the press as a political institution. It was charged with the duty of keeping government from overstepping its bounds. In the words of Jefferson, it was to provide that check on government which no other institution could provide.

Libertarian theorists assumed that out of a multiplicity of voices of the press, some information reaching the public would be false and some opinions unsound. Nevertheless, the state did not have the right to restrict that which it considered false and unsound. If it did, it would inevitably tend to suppress that which was critical of the state or which was contrary to the opinions of government officials. The alternative procedure, as espoused by the libertarians, was to let the public at large be subjected to a barrage of information and opinion, some of it possibly true, some of it possibly false, and some of it containing elements of both. Ultimately the public could be trusted to digest the whole, to discard that not in the public interest and to accept that which served the needs of the individual and of the society of which he is a part. This was the well-known "self-righting" process.

The libertarians also assumed that in a democratic society there would be a multiplicity of voices available to, if not actually reaching, the public. Let every man who has something to say on public issues express himself regardless of whether what he has to say is true or false, and let the public ultimately decide. At no time in history was this assumption completely in accord with the facts. Some men had superior abilities for verbal expression; some men had the interest, energy and drive to express themselves; and some had more direct access to public audiences than others. But theoretically all had the same opportunity if not the same ability or the same means of access.

The libertarians opposed government monopolies of the avenues of communication. They argued that anyone, citizen or alien, who had the inclination should have the unrestricted opportunity to own and operate a unit of mass communication. The field was open to all. It was also assumed that the mass media would operate in a capitalistic society in which free enterprise was a guiding principle. This meant that the instruments of communication would be privately owned and would compete in an open market. Anyone with sufficient capital could start a communication enterprise, and his success or failure would depend upon his ability to produce a profit. Profit, in fact, depended upon his ability to satisfy his customers. In the end, the success of the enterprise would be determined by the public which it sought to serve.

The problem of the economic support of the mass media was never squarely faced by libertarian theorists. They were opposed to government support since it led to domination, and they trusted the capitalist system of private enterprise to find a way. The different media have in the course of history developed different methods of support. The early printed media, especially books, relied almost solely on direct sales of the product to customers. The purchaser provided the economic base. This practice has continued in the book and motion picture industries. The early newspapers and magazines soon discovered a lucrative source of revenue from the sale of "notices" or advertisements, and thus developed an additional function for the press, to stimulate consumption and sell products. The growth of advertising as an important source of economic support for the press was particularly noticeable in Great Britain and in America, and in these countries newspapers and magazines were most free from government domination. Other areas of the globe which were less advanced industrially and in which consumer goods were less widely distributed faced greater difficulties in developing advertising revenues. Cultural differences also played a part in expanding the sales function of the mass media. As a result, economic support in some countries was primarily derived from direct sales to the consumer or in some instances from subsidies supplied by outside interests. The economic support of contemporary media is discussed later in this chapter; but it may be said here that under libertarian theories anyone with economic means can enter the communications field, and his survival depends on his ability to satisfy the needs and wants of his consumers in the face of competition from other units seeking the same market.

What, then, are the principal controls operating on the mass media in a democratic society? Despite all that has been said, the state through its various instrumentalities cannot avoid taking some part in the communications process. Libertarians recognize this fact, but they contend that the less government becomes involved the better. Thus is raised the perennial problem of the extent to which government should be allowed to participate. The state generally operates the postal system through which some of the media are distributed. In many countries the state also operates the telephone and telegraph systems through which it has the opportunity of imposing regulations. The state controls imports and exports, and above all, the state imposes taxes. Through any of these instruments, the state could impose special restrictions on the mass media.

In most democratic societies, the chief instrument of control is the judicial system. In the United States the courts are paramount since they not only apply the law of the land to the press but also determine when the other branches of government are overstepping their authority in imposing restrictions which might contravene constitutional protections. In the last analysis, under our constitutional system the courts determine the limits to which government may go in exercising the authority over the mass media. In other democratic countries, tradition or the legislature performs this function.

In the place of state supervision, libertarian theory provides for a more informal type of control through the self-righting process and through the free competition in the market place of information, opinions, and entertainment. The principal function of the state is to maintain a stable framework within which the free forces of individualism may interact. At times this interaction may be chaotic and the results unproductive. Nevertheless, in the long run this process is to be preferred to authoritarian direction.

The most persistent problem facing democratic societies is determining proper limitations to freedom of expression in the mass media. As has been indicated, all libertarian philosophers agree that freedom of expression is not absolute but limited. What restrictions, then, can be imposed within the framework of democracy without violating liberal doctrines? Unfortunately, no general principles have been developed to assist in solving the problem. The only guide is the historical acceptance of specific limitations without the assistance of a unifying concept.

Professor Zechariah Chafee has listed some of the methods which have been used to control or suppress the mass media: the requirement that books or other publications be licensed in advance, censorship of offending material before publication or while publication is under way, seizure of offending material, injunctions against the publication of a newspaper or book or of specified matter therein, surety bonds against libels or other offending publications, compulsory disclosure of ownership and authorship, postpublication criminal penalties for objectionable matter, postpublication collection of damages in a civil action, postpublication correction of libels and other misstatements, discrimination in access to news sources and facilities, special prohibitions and restrictions on the foreign language press, discrimination and denial in the use of communications facilities for distribution, interference with importation, copyright protection or the denial thereof, taxes, discriminatory subsidies, interference with buying, reading, or listening (40:62-68).

Several types of limitations on the freedom of the press have been universally accepted as being consistent with libertarian principles. All democratic governments recognize the duty of the state to protect the reputations of individuals. Some states perform this duty more assiduously than others, but all recognize the need to restrict the mass media from injuring members of society by defamation. Protection for the individual is usually provided by law and administered by the courts. Innumerable subtleties have engrafted themselves onto the law of defamation and have resulted, in many instances, in enforcement difficulties. Cultural differences may also affect the operation of the law of defamation by placing reliance within a particular culture on substitute methods of protecting individual reputations. A particularly difficult problem arises when damaging words are applied to an individual who is also a public official. Under libertarian doctrines, as an individual he should be protected but as a public official he should be open to public criticism. Here again several unworkable distinctions were attempted by the early nineteenth-century courts. The end result is that in the United States both public officers and candidates for public office find little protection in the law of defamation.

Another commonly accepted restraint on the press is the prohibition against the dissemination of obscene and indecent materials. No sound basic principles have been developed to support the laws against obscenity other than that such restraints are necessary to protect morality. Morality itself is difficult to define, and both courts and legislatures have struggled for several centuries to arrive at an acceptable definition of obscenity. The definition of obscenity has usually been determined by an aggressive minority or by some judge's estimate of the current state of morality. Although some libertarians argue against all types of control based on obscenity, the majority agree that the state has an obligation to protect society, or at least some parts of it, from lewd and indecent publications.

More than two centuries of argument have been devoted to the right of the state to protect itself against the dissemination of information and opinion which might disparage it or undermine it among its adherents. The authoritarians gave a direct and unequivocal answer to the problem (Chapter 1, p. 22), but for the libertarians the solution is not so simple. As noted in the previous chapter, the authoritarians recognized the right of the state to protect its reputation, just as the libertarians conceded the right of the individual to his protection from defamatory publications.

Although the common law of England provided a basis for punishing reflections on the government, this law was never congenial to the American temperament. American independence was accomplished with the aid of both reasoned and vituperative attacks on the British colonial authorities in which many prominent Americans took part. These same Americans, when they framed a government of their own, were predisposed to recognize the value of uninhibited criticism of public officials and public affairs. The revolutionists generally understood that the old law of seditious libel was no longer in effect in the new republic. However, as the leaders settled down to the difficult day-by-day operation of a government covering a wide geographical territory and dispersed population, the task of maintaining authority made officials inclined to revert to traditional attitudes and practices.

Many of the newly established state governments revived the common law of seditious libel, particularly during the tense partisanship of political campaigns. Because of its federal nature, the national government was unable to apply the English criminal law. Therefore it turned to legislation for its protection in times of stress and insecurity. The Alien and Sedition Law of 1798 was an attempt to give the government the power to protect itself from unwarranted criticism. The administration of the law by the Federalists for partisan political purposes conflicted with the deep-seated democratic principles of the American public. As a result, no further attempts were made in this direction throughout the nineteenth century. The individual states gradually abandoned the English doctrine of seditious libel, and by the time Jacksonian democracy took over, the law was obsolete.

The characteristic of the libertarian concept of the function of the press in society which distinguishes it from the other theories discussed in this volume is the right and duty of the press to serve as an extralegal check on government. The press was to keep officers of the state from abusing or exceeding their authority. It was to be the watchdog over the workings of democracy, ever vigilant to spot and expose any arbitrary or authoritarian practice. And to fulfill this function adequately, the press had to be completely free from control or domination by those elements which it was to guard against. Because liberalism was forced to struggle for several centuries against authoritarianism, it considered the established government its greatest enemy. Governmental authority, however, could be made to serve the interests of liberalism if strong and effective checks on its use could be found. The press was an instrument which, together with other safeguards, could fulfill this function. Under traditional authoritarianism as well as under the Russian-Soviet Communist system, the interests of the people were theoretically identified with the interests of the state. Therefore what liberals called a "check on government" was to the authoritarians merely an attempt to impede or interfere with the accomplishment of the objectives of the state.

Although the founders of the American system of government held the political function of the press to be paramount, other activities important to the adequate functioning of a democratic society were also assigned to the mass media. The media were envisaged as the principal instruments for adult education. They were to be the avenues by which the general public received information and discussion on matters of public importance. The federal postal system was no sooner set up than reduced rates were authorized to encourage the growth of newspapers and periodicals. The success of democracy was posited upon an intelligent and informed electorate, and the mass media along with public schools were charged with providing the public with educational materials. The media were to contribute to the development of arts and sciences, to the elevation of public tastes, and to improvements in the practical business of daily living. The authoritarians did not disagree with assigning educational functions to the press, since under their system both educational institutions and the mass media were to be guided by the same principle — the accomplishment of the objectives of the state.

THE PRESS IN MODERN LIBERTARIAN THEORY

We now turn from the theory behind the functioning of the press under libertarian principles to a discussion of the operation of the mass media in contemporary society. Great Britain, the United States, and some of the British Dominions follow a common pattern in what has been described as the Anglo-American tradition. A number of the younger democratic countries have tried to imitate or transplant this tradition with varying degrees of success, and their failures and accomplishments will be discussed later in this chapter. Let us look at the operation of the mass media in the United States.

The twentieth century has been faced with the problem of applying the libertarian theory to contemporary problems of the mass media. Whatever contribution has been made has grown out of experiences in two world wars and out of the development and expansion of the new media of communication such as motion pictures and broadcasting.

During the two world wars, the immediate problem was to establish principles governing the dissemination of expressions which might interfere with the immediate objective of the government — winning the war. Pure libertarian doctrine made no provision for the cataclysmic effects of a world-wide war or, for that matter, a local war. In a vague way, libertarians had granted that a government had the right to protect itself from destruction under special circumstances, but they had made no reasoned analysis of how far a state might go in curtailing liberty of expression in wartime. During World War I, the government set up a system for censoring outgoing and incoming messages, but it made no attempt to muzzle the mass media within the territorial boundaries of the United States. A system of voluntary censorship was put into operation with the cooperation of the mass media, principally the newspapers and magazines. The same system with improved procedures was adopted during World War II, this time including radio.

An important contribution growing out of wartime experiences was the attempt by the Supreme Court of the United States to define the limits of free discussion in a democracy. Members of the court recognized that under special conditions such as a major war the traditional freedoms of the individual must yield to the immediate objective. The problem was to find a formula that would preserve as much of the libertarian concept of freedom as possible while permitting the state to carry out its program without undue interference or obstruction. Authoritarian governments were, of course, unconcerned about this problem, but for libertarian governments it was a serious and confusing issue. During the war, the Supreme Court took the position that if there was a *reasonable tendency* for discussion to obstruct the war effort, such discussion could be declared a crime and its participants punished. Liberal thinkers and legal scholars rushed to criticize the court for departing from traditional libertarian principles, and shortly after the war the court changed its mind by adopting the formula originally proposed by Justices Brandeis and Holmes. Justice Holmes introduced the formula in the Schenck case in these words: "The question in every case is whether the words used are used in such circumstances and are of such a nature as to create a clear and present danger that they will bring about the substantive evils that Congress has a right to prevent. It is a question of proximity and degree" (57:52).

This formula has become known as the *clear and present danger test*. Both Holmes and Brandeis recognized the need for some restriction on freedom of speech and press during national emergencies. Their formula was an attempt to provide a principle which would determine the bounds of free discussion on one hand and the restrictive powers of government on the other. They rejected the "reasonable tendency" test in favor of one which would allow a wider latitude of freedom. They granted the government the right to punish anyone who exceeded the bounds of freedom, and they set those bounds to cover as wide an area as possible. Their solution was to restrict government interference with freedom of expression except under circumstances where there was an urgent danger to the objectives of the state. And not only must the danger be urgent but the possibility that the discussion might adversely affect the objectives of the state must be immediate. The "clear and present danger test" became the basis for determining the validity of most attempts to curtail freedom of speech and of the press since World War I.

Alexander Meiklejohn has vigorously criticized the test as inconsistent with libertarian principles. He argues that discussion by members of the public should have the same immunity from government interference as that of members of the legislature who in their debates are not subject to a "clear and present danger test." He also attempts to differentiate between the "liberty" of the First Amendment and the "liberty" of the Fifth Amendment. The liberty of the First Amendment, he argues, is a public right (by which he apparently means one enforceable by the public) which is unabridgable. The liberty of the Fifth Amendment is a private right (one enforceable by the individual) which can be limited by government under "due process" (51:35-41).[4]

The Supreme Court of the United States has also approved legislative proposals to penalize discussions advocating the overthrow of the democratic system of government by force and violence. The problem under libertarian governments was to draw the line between discussions of the relative merits of the Communist and capitalist systems and agitation or advocacy which sought to supplant the existing state by revolutionary methods. The phrase "by force and violence" has been introduced into restrictive legislation by both the federal government and many of the states. This legislation has been used to silence some of the Communist Party officials, but it has not been employed to suppress Communist Party organs such as the *Daily Worker*. This type of statute when coupled with the "clear and present danger test" has been accepted by the Supreme Court as a constitutional method of dealing with persons who seek to overthrow the democratic capitalist system. However, libertarians are concerned over the problem of preserving free discussion under traditional principles when fear and hysteria may affect the climate of public opinion.

The Supreme Court, particularly when Charles Evans Hughes was Chief Justice, followed basic libertarian principles in a number of decisions affecting the freedom of the mass media. Among the restrictions it declared unconstitutional were the Minnesota injunction against the further publication of a political scandal-sheet (283 U.S. 697, 1931) and a Louisiana tax on the gross receipts of large newspapers which opposed the Huey Long regime (297 U.S. 233, 1936). Subsequently the Supreme Court has restricted the powers of inferior courts to punish newspapers for contempt of court for publications

---

[4] The clear and present danger test is also discussed and criticized in a series of articles by Chester J. Antieau in 29 and 30.

which might interfere with the administration of justice (314 U.S. 252, 1941), and it has struck down legislative attempts to limit the circulation of publications devoted to "crime and bloodshed" (335 U.S. 507, 1948). The unique function of the Supreme Court under the American system is to evaluate all types of limitations on freedom of speech and of the press which emanate from government sources. Practically no other democratic government seems to have adopted this device for protecting the mass media from the encroachments by government.

The printed media, being the first on the scene, have been most active in the struggle to establish libertarian principles of freedom. Newspapers, particularly, led in the battle against attempts by the state to reduce their status and limit their functions. With the establishment of a theoretical basis for the modern concept of freedom of expression, the press developed what has been called "the theory of objective reporting" to fulfill its function as an information medium. This theory, which originated some time in the nineteenth century, was widely acclaimed in the United States and Great Britain as a unique contribution to journalism during the first quarter of the twentieth century. Its origin in America may be traced to the growth of cooperative news-gathering associations which furnished the local newspaper with information from state, national, and international sources. Most newspapers were then violently partisan, and they resented attempts to induce them to publish materials favorable to, or slanted in the direction of, the opposition party. The alternative was to eliminate as far as possible all political bias in the news. The news agencies instructed reporters and writers to remember that their writings were being distributed to both Democratic and Republican clients and had to be acceptable to both. Writers became adept at constructing nonpartisan accounts, and from this practice grew the concept of objective reporting which has permeated American journalism to the present.

The spread of objective reporting throughout American journalism was accelerated by the decline in political partisanship in the press and by the change of the newspaper from opinion journal to news medium. The growth of advertising and the drive to increase circulations also contributed to the general acceptance of the ideal of objectivity. Newspaper reporters thought that their job required an attitude of aloofness. They became spectators rather than participants in the controversies of the day. They carefully avoided any appearance of partisanship or evaluation. News was a raw account; opinions were to be sharply separated from it and in most American newspapers relegated to the editorial page. The theory of objective reporting became a matter of professional pride among American journalists, who held that reporting the "facts of the day" was their only duty. In many countries professing libertarian principles, the theory failed to find general acceptance, and in countries where the press was tied to political parties the ideal of objectivity failed to flourish.

In recent years objective reporting has been severely criticized on the ground that it neglects to tell the whole truth and that it fails to give the reader a sufficient basis for evaluating the news in terms of social goals. These criticisms are discussed more fully in the succeeding chapter on the social responsibility theory of the press.

Another problem of journalism which involves libertarian concepts and which the press has avidly pursued in recent years is the right of access to government sources of information. The contest to report the debates of the British Parliament was discussed earlier in this chapter (p. 48). The early American constitutional conventions were closed to both public and reporters. As the nineteenth century advanced, the press was able to point out the logical necessity under democratic theory of a complete report of governmental activities to the public. Although logical theory supported the news media, the practical problem of implementing the theory presented obstacles. The task of telling the public what government at all levels was doing was not too difficult in the early years of the present century. Government was conducted by a relatively small number of officials, and its activities were principally legislative or judicial. However, during the second quarter of this century, a tremendous expansion took place both in the activities of government and in the number of its personnel. This was particularly true in the administrative area. Practically no aspect of life today is exempt from government participation at either the national, state, or local level, and the pervasiveness of this participation has intensified the problem of reporting the contemporary scene to the American public.

Such reporting is particularly difficult at the national level, where government activities have expanded at an impressive rate. The tradition of secrecy derived from authoritarian precedents has always been most pronounced in the area of foreign affairs, which are normally under the jurisdiction of national governments. Although reporters and correspondents have been permitted to attend the sessions of legislative bodies for generations, they do not have the same degree of access to administrative officers or groups. News representatives have seldom been allowed to sit in on diplomatic sessions.

Unfortunately no general principles have been developed to indicate when and where the public has a legitimate interest in public affairs, and consequently newsmen have had very little guidance. Since the Department of State or the Foreign Office could refuse to reveal its activities, why could not other offices of the government? And if the federal government could refuse access to information, why could not the state and local governments? Libertarian theory assumed that the government's business was the public's business. Yet impressive arguments can be advanced for denying the public or its representatives access to some government proceedings or records.

Since World War II the problem of restricting information which might affect the military security of the nation has been exceedingly troublesome both to government officials and representatives of the press. What types of information should be classified and by whom continues to be debated. And what check can be placed on the classifiers to see that they are not overzealous in carrying out their functions? The problem becomes particularly acute when decisions are made on withholding scientific information which might possibly be useful to a potential enemy. Also, many government activities impinge upon the privacy of the individual. Does the public at large have the right to know how much income tax an individual citizen pays? Do newsmen have the right to sit in on conferences in the state department or committees of Congress? Should they be permitted to attend the meetings of the local county board or the board of education?

Libertarian theory has not been able as yet to answer these perplexing questions. The mass media through their professional organizations have contended that all government business should be open to them and that they as purveyors of information to the public have both the obligation and the right to gather and transmit news about government activities at all levels.

MOTION PICTURES IN CURRENT LIBERTARIANISM

The newer media, including motion pictures and the various forms of broadcasting, have forced the libertarian theorist to face a host of novel and complex problems. The original democratic solutions to the problem of the function of the mass media were based largely on the political contributions of the printed media. When entertainment was added to the political function and when methods of reaching a mass audience other than through the printed word were developed, libertarian theory was confronted with the need for adjustment.

The motion picture as a mass medium is a product of the twentieth century. Because of its similarities and association with the legitimate theater, its place in the social structure has followed that which had been assigned to the stage. Authoritarian theory had assumed that the state had complete control of the theater. Sixteenth- and seventeenth-century governments established the right, if not always the practice, of strictly regulating entertainment on political and religious as well as on moral grounds. (See 45.) The Protestant Reformation produced no great and persuasive argument for freedom of the theater as it did in John Milton's plea for freedom of the press. Consequently, libertarian theory either ignored the problem or, because of its non-political characteristics, assumed that it was unimportant. The advent of the motion picture with its ability to reach vast audiences and to produce profound effects on these audiences has forced a re-examination of the bases of libertarian theory. Theaters had been licensed and plays censored for generations; motion pictures were merely an extension of the theater and therefore subject to licensing and censorship by the authorities. This reasoning was applied to the early attempts to establish official censorship boards and received the approval of the Supreme Court of the United States in 1915.[5]

Since World War I, the motion picture has clearly shared the function of furnishing information and opinion as well as entertainment on which citizens build their attitudes and convictions and upon which, in part, they base their behavior. The newsreel is an informational medium. Documentary films, now produced in considerable volume, perform both informational and educational functions. The analogy with the theater has decreased and the similarities with the press have increased as the motion picture has expanded its news and opinion offerings. Unlike the newspaper, the motion picture industry has not battled vigorously for its rights — at least not until recently. Producers cooperated with both official and unofficial regulatory agencies. The industry as a whole tried to regulate its more recalcitrant members through a voluntary Production Code under the aus-

---

[5] The most comprehensive account of the problems of the motion picture industry is that contained in *Freedom of the Movies*, by Ruth A. Inglis (47).

pices of the Motion Picture Producers and Distributors of America.

Why should the motion picture be subject to licensing and censorship while the printed media are free from these restrictions? This was the question which faced the government and libertarian theorists. Granted that the movies were primarily entertainment, granted that they reached a relatively youthful segment of the population, granted that they were capable of debasing moral standards, nevertheless were they not an important institution in democratic society and should they not also be tested on the basis of libertarian principles? As Miss Inglis has pointed out: "The problem as regards the movies is only an individual instance of the general question which has puzzled philosophers and statesmen for centuries: How can the public will prevail and order be maintained and, at the same time, dissident minorities have their proper influence for change? The problem is one of devising social mechanisms for achieving these results" (47:173).

The Commission on Freedom of the Press, headed by Robert M. Hutchins, after a careful and considered study of the problem of the motion picture in a democratic society, made the following recommendation: "The constitutional guarantees of freedom of the press should be recognized as including motion pictures. The growing importance of the documentary film gives fresh emphasis to the need" (47:vi).

But giving the motion picture status under the constitutional guarantees does not finally solve the problem. Even if one accepts the proposition that the movies should enjoy the traditional libertarian freedoms, the question remains as to what if any regulations can be imposed upon the medium. The Supreme Court of the United States took a significant step in answering this question by eliminating some of the more objectionable standards under which official motion picture censors operate on the ground that they were too vague for satisfactory administration (36). In the United States at least, the motion picture is rapidly being accepted as a medium worthy of being encompassed by the traditional libertarian concept of freedom of expression, and progress is being made toward achieving this end.

BROADCASTING IN LIBERTARIAN THEORY

Broadcasting, including both radio and television, is the youngest of the mass media of communication and has presented libertarian theory with many perplexing problems. In its early phases, the transmission of messages by radio resembled in many respects the telephone and telegraph systems. These latter were generally considered to be outside the sphere of mass communications since they were merely point-to-point transmission systems which took no account of the character of the messages which they transmitted. The telephone and telegraph were by nature monopolistic and consequently subject to government regulation as common carriers. Libertarian doctrines accepted governmental regulation or operation of these transmission monopolies "in the public interest." When point-to-point radio arrived, it was automatically endowed with the characteristics of a common carrier and subjected to the same type of control.

Broadcasting, however, was something different from the mere transmission of messages by radio. Here, in fact, was a new mass medium capable of reaching a vast audience simultaneously. It was concerned not only with the transmission of messages but with the content of those messages. To this extent it resembled newspapers, magazines, and motion pictures. On the other hand, it utilized electromagnetic waves, of which there is a limited supply. Obviously not everyone could establish a radio broadcasting station without producing complete chaos on the air waves. Regulation was necessary if only for the allocation of frequencies.

Libertarian societies have solved the problem of broadcasting in various ways. Some like France have established government-owned and -operated monopolies following the precedent of telephone and telegraph carriers. Others have adopted the British model, which is based on a public corporation only indirectly responsible to the government in power. In the United States, the solution has been a system of private ownership under allocation and regulation by a federal commission created by the Congress. Canada has attempted to operate a dual system under which a public corporation operates the national stations and private enterprise the local stations.

Although the American system of broadcasting is more consistent with libertarian principles than the others, it faces the problem of adjusting traditional doctrines of freedom with the physical facts of broadcasting. A government agency is a necessary and obvious solution to the problem of allocating frequencies. On what basis should it make these allocations? The standard adopted was one which had been used for some time in the common-carrier field — the standard of "public interest, convenience and necessity." This was a vague standard, but apparently it was the best that Congress could provide under the circumstances. It had been used as a basis for regulating railroads, power companies, and telephone and telegraph companies, and was an obvious choice for broadcasting.

The Federal Communications Commission, established in 1934 as the successor to the Federal Radio Commission (1927), undertook putting the standard into practice. How was it to determine that an assignment of a segment of the electromagnetic spectrum to Applicant A would better serve the "public interest, convenience and necessity" than an assignment to Applicant B or C? The other mass media were private enterprises established at the will of the entrepreneur. In fact, a government license to operate was abhorrent to libertarian principles. Such a device struck at the very basis of the effectiveness of the medium as a check on government and its officials. But no other alternative was apparently available for broadcasting; and the Commission, faced with the necessity of issuing licenses, searched for some reasonable ground on which to base its decisions. It almost inevitably took the position that, since the air waves were a natural resource of limited capacity, their assignment must be based, in part at least, on program content. Public interest would be served if all segments of the population were able to receive the best possible radio and television programs. An agency of the government was now definitely passing judgment on the content of the medium. The broadcasting industry objected vigorously that this interpretation of the function of the Commission violated the traditional libertarian principles of freedom of speech and of the press. Broadcasting, the industry contended, was not the same as a telephone company; it was more like a newspaper or a magazine with some aspects of the theater and the motion picture industry thrown in. Armed with the slogan, "radio as free as the press," the broadcasters argued that the function of government was solely to assign frequencies and not to regulate program content.

The Commission's position was set out in a now famous document, the *Blue Book*. In that document, the Commission asserted that standards of performance must necessarily be considered in frequency allocation, otherwise the occupant would acquire a vested interest in public property, and it specified some of the attributes of adequate programming. A full-blown debate followed the publication of the *Blue Book*, but no permanent conclusions were reached. Neither the Congress nor the Supreme Court has seen fit to resolve the issue. The court has indicated that broadcasting comes under the protection of the constitutional guarantees of freedom of expression, but it also has taken the position that the government through the Federal Communications Commission has the right not only to supervise the use of the air waves but also to determine the composition of the traffic on those waves.

The question of the economic support has added to the complexity of the problem of broadcasting. Some libertarian democracies have provided for direct government subsidies; others have set up a system of taxation on the use of receiving sets; and others like the United States have relied on advertising revenues. Since economic support can seriously affect the performance of an instrument of mass communication, the problem of the extent of the dependence on state support becomes a serious one. The high cost of television operation has tended to increase rather than decrease the seriousness of the issue. How can a medium dependent on state funds remain immune to government influence? Advertising revenues offer an alternative, but to what extent will they debase or standardize radio and television performance?

Libertarian theory has not yet solved the problems of motion pictures and broadcasting. It has set a broad framework within which the new media are seeking to adjust themselves. The answers will probably be found through experimentation and experience, through trial and error, as well as through a more careful analysis of the theoretical functions of the new media. As it has done in the past, libertarian philosophy is muddling through, postponing any final decisions until it is sure that it is on the right track.

THE LIBERTARIAN PRESS ELSEWHERE IN THE WORLD

The United States and Great Britain have been the chief custodians of libertarian principles for more than a century, but other countries of the world have to a greater or lesser extent adopted these same principles. As the democratic form of government spread throughout the world, the concept of freedom of speech and press followed as an integral part of the libertarian doctrine. In some countries the concept found a fertile soil; in many others it was planted with a great flourish and with high expectations but in a short time withered and died. In others the seed produced a variation that showed little resemblance to the Anglo-American variety.

Many of the underdeveloped areas of the world found it particularly difficult to transplant the western ideals of a free press. In many instances the ideal was accepted with enthusiasm, but internal conditions apparently were not conducive to the full development of democratic principles. Nationalistic pressures, internal security and economic conditions were the principal factors which made it difficult to implement libertarian theories.

Constitutional protections for the mass media have generally been adopted by the newer democracies which have been established since World War I. The constitution of the Philippine Islands (1935) contains a simple statement: "Article 8, No law shall be passed abridging freedom of speech or of the press, or the right of the people peaceably to assemble and petition the government for redress of grievances." The constitution of Israel (1948) is more elaborate: "Article 16, Freedom of speech and the free expression of opinion in writing or in any other form are guaranteed. This constitutional guarantee shall not extend to utterances of publications which are libelous, slanderous, or obscene, or which are designed to stir up racial or religious hatred, or to incite to violence or crime, or which advocate the suppression of human rights, or of the democratic system of government, or which reveal secrets of national defense. The institution of a preventive censorship shall be unlawful save in time of war or national emergency and shall require specific legislative authorization and be subject to continuous parliamentary control and review."

Despite the spread of democratic principles, some nations which have officially adopted libertarian protections against government control of the press have reverted to authoritarian practices whenever a domestic political crisis arises. Both Argentina and Colombia have adopted traditional constitutional protections for their press, but both have on occasions ignored these provisions and suppressed objectionable publications. (For a recent example in Colombia, see 43:36.)

In the later stages of World War II, libertarians had high hopes that democratic principles of free speech and press would spread throughout the world when the war ended and an effective international organization was established. They were confident that in an international arena they could effectively cope with the principles of authoritarianism and Communism. One of the motivating forces behind the establishment of the United Nations was the world-wide recognition of "fundamental human rights" in the libertarian tradition. One of these basic human rights was freedom of expression or, as it later came to be known under tutelage of American experts, "freedom of information."

The task of defining and implementing these human rights throughout the world was assigned to the General Assembly of the United Nations, to the Economic and Social Council, and to a special Commission on Human Rights. The Commission on Human Rights set up a Sub-Commission on Freedom of Information and the Press which tackled specific problems of the mass media of communication. At a United Nations Conference on Freedom of Information in Geneva in 1948, the authoritarians, libertarians, and Communists presented arguments for their particular doctrines on the function of the mass media in society. In spite of the apparent difficulties of reconciling the divergent points of view, leaders in the United Nations hoped that some agreement could be reached. Succeeding conferences and meetings of the Sub-Commission studied particular problems, such as the adequacy of news available to the peoples of the world, the obstacles to a free flow of information, an international code of ethics for information personnel, the jamming of radio broadcasts, the free transmission of newsreels, the newsprint problem, and discriminatory treatment of foreign information personnel.

In the meantime the General Assembly drafted a Convention on the International Transmission of News and the Right of Correction which was approved but not opened for signatures pending the completion of a draft of a Convention on Freedom of Information. Here at last the machinery broke down, as it appeared impossible to reconcile the divergent points of view. The principal antagonists were the United States on one side and Soviet Russia on the other. In between were the small nations which were unwilling to accept the principles of either libertarianism or Communism. No apparent progress has been made in the last several years toward solving the problem of information agencies on a world-wide basis.

In analyzing the causes of the difficulties encountered, the rapporteur on freedom of information of the Economic and Social Council has written in his 1954 report:

Fundamental to most of the debates on freedom of information and a main factor in retarding progress has been the marked difference of opinion regarding the rights and freedoms as against the duties and responsibilities involved in the concept of freedom of information. It would however be an oversimplification to reduce the difference to a conflict between the thesis that the interests of organized society are most effectively advanced by an unrestricted access to the market-place of ideas, and the thesis that such interests are better safeguarded by state control and indoctrination. The actual situation in the world may be more accurately described as a "con-

tinuous ideological spectrum," with all the various countries ranged somewhere between two extremes. This "spectrum" has been observed during
practically all discussions on freedom of information since 1946 (50:11).

SUMMARY

The libertarian theory of the function of the mass media in a democratic society has had a long and arduous history. This history has
paralleled the development of democratic principles in government
and free enterprise in economics. The theory itself can trace a re-
spected lineage among the philosophers of ancient times, but it
received its greatest impetus from the developments in western
Europe in the sixteenth and seventeenth centuries. From Milton to
Holmes it has stressed the superiority of the principle of individual
freedom and judgment and the axiom that truth when allowed free
rein will emerge victorious from any encounter. Its slogans have been
the "self-righting process" and the "free market place of ideas." It
has been an integral part of the great march of democracy which has
resulted in the stupendous advancement of the well-being of humanity.
It has been the guiding principle of western civilization for more than
two hundred years.

In recent years the libertarian theory has been subjected to search-
ing criticisms. Some of these are set forth in the following chapter on
the theory of social responsibility. It has been pointed out that some
of the underlying axioms of the theory are far from sound. Rationalism
has been under fire, particularly by modern psychologists; the theory
of natural rights has been exposed as merely a persuasive slogan without basic political or social foundations; free enterprise has been questioned as an economic philosophy; and the right of the individual to
jeopardize the welfare of the majority has been forcefully attacked.

Carl Becker has aptly summarized some of the current confusion:

What confuses our purposes and defeats our hopes is that the simple concepts upon which the Age of Enlightenment relied with assurance have lost
for us their universal and infallible quality. Natural law turns out to be no
more than a convenient and temporary hypothesis. Imprescriptible rights
have such validity only as prescriptive law confers upon them. Liberty, once
identified with emancipation of the individual from governmental restraint,
is now seen to be inseparable from the complex pattern of social regulation.
Even the sharp, definitive lines of reason and truth are blurred. Reason, we
suspect, is a function of the animal organism, and truth no more than the
perception of discordant experience pragmatically adjusted for a particular
purpose and for the time being (32:93).

In spite of such questionings, libertarianism has demonstrated its theoretical and practical advantages. It has struck off the manacles from the mind of man, and it has opened up new vistas for humanity. Its greatest defect has been its failure to provide rigorous standards for the day-to-day operations of the mass media — in short, a stable formula to distinguish between liberty and abuse of liberty. It is vague, inconclusive, and sometimes inconsistent. Its greatest assets, however, are its flexibility, its adaptability to change, and above all its confidence in its ability to advance the interests and welfare of human beings by continuing to place its trust in individual self-direction.

THE SOCIAL RESPONSIBILITY

THEORY OF

THE PRESS

THEODORE PETERSON *3*

Today, when newspaper publishers speak about their calling, such phrases as "the public's right to know" and "the public responsibility of the press" are likely to creep into their talk. Such ideas and the press performance resulting from them represent an important modification of traditional libertarian theory, for nothing in libertarian theory established the public's right to information or required the publisher to assume moral responsibilities. A fairly valid expression of the publisher's position under libertarian theory was that attributed to William Peter Hamilton of the *Wall Street Journal:* "A newspaper is a private enterprise owing nothing whatever to the public, which grants it no franchise. It is therefore affected with no public interest. It is emphatically the property of the owner, who is selling a manufactured product at his own risk. . . ."

THE THEORY IN BRIEF

The twentieth century, however, brought a gradual shift away from pure libertarianism, and in its place began to emerge what has been called the "social responsibility theory of the press." Just what do we mean by "social responsibility theory"? Later, when we compare the theory with libertarian theory, we will see it in full dimension and in full implication. But for an understanding of just what we are talking about, let us here sketch the theory in general outline. The theory has this major premise: Freedom carries concomitant obligations; and the press, which enjoys a privileged position under our government, is obliged to be responsible to society for carrying out certain essential functions of mass communication in contemporary society. To the extent that the press recognizes its responsibilities and makes them the basis of operational policies, the libertarian system will satisfy the needs of society. To the extent that the press does not assume its responsibilities, some other agency must see that the essential functions of mass communication are carried out.

The functions of the press under social responsibility theory are basically the same as those under libertarian theory. Six tasks came to be ascribed to the press as traditional theory evolved: (1) servicing the political system by providing information, discussion, and debate on public affairs; (2) enlightening the public so as to make it capable of self-government; (3) safeguarding the rights of the individual by serving as a watchdog against government; (4) servicing the economic system, primarily by bringing together the buyers and sellers of goods and services through the medium of advertising; (5) providing entertainment; (6) maintaining its own financial self-sufficiency so as to be free from the pressures of special interests.

The social responsibility theory in general accepts those six functions. But it reflects a dissatisfaction with the interpretation of those functions by some media owners and operators and with the way in which the press has carried them out. Social responsibility theory accepts the role of the press in servicing the political system, in enlightening the public, in safeguarding the liberties of the individual; but it represents the opinion that the press has been deficient in performing those tasks. It accepts the role of the press in servicing the economic system, but it would not have this task take precedence over such other functions as promoting the democratic processes or enlightening the public. It accepts the role of the press in furnishing entertainment but with the proviso that the entertainment be "good" entertainment. It accepts the need for the press as an institution to remain financially self-supporting, but if necessary it would exempt certain individual media from having to earn their way in the market place.

ROOTS OF THE THEORY

Just as libertarian theory was a composite of ideas, so the emerging social responsibility theory has grown out of the ideas of many persons. Men who have contributed component ideas to it might abhor the theory as a whole — just as, say, John Milton, who contributed the idea of the self-righting process to libertarian theory, no doubt would have found fault with libertarian theory in its full form.

The social responsibility theory still is largely a grafting of new ideas onto traditional theory. However, the Commission on Freedom of the Press in its various books after World War II did a great deal toward making social responsibility a new, integrated theory instead of a mere appendage to the traditional one. Especially important to the idea of social responsibility were *A Free and Responsible Press* by the Commission as a whole and *Freedom of the Press: A Framework of Principle* by William E. Hocking, a member of the Commission. Even members of the Commission were not in unanimous accord, since some of them hugged tradition and others stood far from it. However, all members did assent to the joint report and to a brief "Summary of Principle."

The developing social responsibility theory, like the libertarian theory which it is replacing, is an Anglo-American concept. About the time that the Commission began issuing its reports in this country, a Royal Commission on the Press, formed at the instigation of the National Union of Journalists, started to study concentration in the press in Britain and to consider means of improving press performance there. Its report supports and supplements the writings of the Commission on Freedom of the Press.

It is important to remember that the social responsibility theory is still chiefly a *theory*. But as a theory it is important because it suggests a direction in which thinking about freedom of the press is heading. Then, too, some aspects of the theory have found their way into practice.

In Britain, on recommendation of the Royal Commission, a General Council of the Press has been formed to encourage a sense of public responsibility and public service in the press. Its main function has been to condemn and publicize questionable practices on the part of the press, to investigate complaints, to seek redress if the complaints are justified, and to reply to them if they are not. Its first annual report, available to the public, included charges against a number of specific newspapers as well as its survey of trends in the press as a whole.

In America, the publishers of several newspapers — the St. Louis *Post-Dispatch,* the Louisville *Courier-Journal,* the Milwaukee *Journal,* the Cowles newspapers of Iowa and Minnesota, to name just a few — seem to feel a strong responsibility to the communities they serve. The movie industry, operating under a system of self-regulation, serves the public interest as it conceives it. The radio and television networks and stations, required by law to serve the public interest, perform in what they take to be the public welfare. Many persons doubtless would remark that there is a large chasm between the genuine public interest and what the movies, radio, and television take it to be. That is not the point. The point is that the self-regulation of the movies and the government regulation of broadcasting represent sharp cleavages with the traditional theory of the press. They are in far closer harmony with social responsibility theory than with libertarian theory.

When the framers of the federal constitution appended an amendment establishing freedom of the press, they had no intention of binding the publisher to certain responsibilities in exchange for his freedom. As Charles Beard has said, freedom of the press meant "the right to be just or unjust, partisan or nonpartisan, true or false, in news columns and editorial column," and truth telling had little or nothing to do with it (77:13). Indeed, the press in the first years of the new United States was characterized by partisanship, invective and unrestraint, and Frank Luther Mott has called the early nineteenth century "the Dark Age of Partisan Journalism." Publishers may have thought that public opinion approved of their excesses, since public opinion had demanded the end of restrictions on the press.

But there was a deeper reason for the free hand which the constitution gave to publishers, one which we will explore in greater detail when we discuss the premises underlying the emergent social responsibility theory of the press. The framers of the constitution were children of the Enlightenment, and their assumptions about the nature of man and the relationship of man to government were implicit in the instrument they drafted. Government was the chief foe of liberty, they believed, and the press must be free to serve as a guardian against governmental encroachments on individual liberty. If the press were free, men would speak. True, they might lie, vilify, distort. But the wonderful invisible hand envisioned by Adam Smith and the self-righting process discerned by John Milton would set things right. Man would seek truth amidst the welter of ideas which swarmed in the market place; and being rational, he would separate truth from false-hood, good from bad.

But somewhere along the way, faith diminished in the optimistic notion that a virtually absolute freedom and the nature of man carried built-in correctives for the press. A rather considerable fraction of articulate Americans began to demand certain standards of perform-ance from the press. They threatened to enact legislation, even did enact it, if the press did not meet certain of those standards. Chiefly of their own volition, publishers began to link responsibility with free-dom. They formulated codes of ethical behavior, and they operated their media with some concern for the public good — the public good as they regarded it, at least. Somewhere along the way, in short, a rationale of social responsibility began to evolve; and to put it into its proper context, let us look at its historical origins before we examine it critically.

TECHNOLOGICAL DEVELOPMENTS BEHIND THE THEORY

The social responsibility theory of the press was born of several things. One was the technological and industrial revolution which changed the face of the nation and the American way of living and which affected the nature of the press itself. Another was the sharp voice of criticism, which spoke often as the media grew in size and importance, and which sometimes carried the tacit threat of govern-ment regulation. Another was a new intellectual climate in which some persons looked with suspicion on the basic assumptions of the Enlightenment. And finally there was the development of a profes-sional spirit as journalism attracted men of principle and education, and as the communications industries reflected the growing sense of social responsibility assumed by American business and industry generally.

The technological and industrial revolution and the social changes which came with it had manifold effects on the press. Technological advances increased the size, speed, and efficiency of the old media and brought new ones — movies, radio, and television. Industrialization was accompanied by a growing volume of advertising, which became the major support of newspapers, magazines, and broadcasting. It also was accompanied by urbanization, and the large numbers of persons brought together helped to make possible newspapers of large circulation. Gains in education and in the number of citizens tremendously expanded the market for products of the press. The press became a ubiquitous instrumentality.

It also became one controlled by a relatively few owners. Technological improvement made it possible for just a few media to serve a vast audience. But the facilities for reaching a large audience were costly. As units of the press became increasingly large and expensive, newcomers found it increasingly difficult to enter the communications industries, and many old-timers failed to survive. Ownership of the media came to be concentrated in comparatively few hands. Daily newspapers steadily decreased in number, and so did the cities with competing papers. Five giant publishers accounted for the great bulk of total magazine circulation and of the total sum spent on magazine advertising. Another five companies produced almost all of the movies which Americans saw. Two or three large networks served virtually all of the broadcasting stations in the nation.

DEVELOPING CRITICISM OF THE PRESS

As the press became a mammoth, pervasive implement of mass communication, it became the object of a good deal of criticism. The first full-length book assailing the press appeared in 1859, and there had been attacks before that; but the criticisms increased in force and intensity in the twentieth century. The themes of twentieth-century criticism, in general, have been these:

1. The press has wielded its enormous power for its own ends. The owners have propagated their own opinions, especially in matters of politics and economics, at the expense of opposing views.

2. The press has been subservient to big business and at times has let advertisers control editorial policies and editorial content.

3. The press has resisted social change.

4. The press has often paid more attention to the superficial and sensational than to the significant in its coverage of current happenings, and its entertainment has often been lacking in substance.

5. The press has endangered public morals.

6. The press has invaded the privacy of individuals without just cause.

7. The press is controlled by one socioeconomic class, loosely the

"business class," and access to the industry is difficult for the new-comer; therefore, the free and open market of ideas is endangered.

Those have been the general indictments against the press as a whole; the specific charges have varied with the times and with the media. Books and magazines have been singled out less frequently, perhaps, than the other media. However, individual books have been damned as corrupters of morals from time to time since the century opened, as were large numbers of inexpensive paper-bound editions in the forties and fifties. Magazines have often been included in blanket criticisms of the press, and an occasional sniper has fired at their low denomi-nator content and at their subservience to the counting room. The shrillest criticism of magazines has been of periodicals on the fringes of the industry — the magazines which traffic in pornography and the comic books, which have been charged with debasing moral standards and with inciting young people to crime.

The lines for much contemporary criticism of the newspaper were laid down in 1911 by Will Irwin in a series of articles in *Collier's* (71). Among other things, Irwin observed that the influence of the news-paper had shifted from its editorials to its news columns; that the commercial nature of the newspaper, not just advertising, was respon-sible for many of its shortcomings; and that entry into the field had become exceedingly difficult for the newcomer.

As advertising became increasingly important to newspapers, it was viewed as a sinister force which tainted the news columns and caused editors to suppress material unfavorable to big advertisers. That was the line taken by Upton Sinclair in *The Brass Check* in 1919 and by George Seldes in *Freedom of the Press* in 1935. Seldes maintained that line in a newsletter, *In Fact,* in the forties, but by then it had become largely discredited; critics recognized that the publisher, as a business-man, might naturally share the attitudes of other businessmen and be influenced by them in the conduct of his newspaper. During the thir-ties, newspaper publishers as businessmen shared in the attacks against business generally, and they were the subjects of such group portraits of "lords of the press" as Harold Ickes' *America's House of Lords* and of such individual portraits as Ferdinand Lundberg's *Imperial Hearst.* In the forties, a major concern was the declining number of dailies in the face of the highest circulations on record, a situation which some observers thought threatened the free flow of ideas.

The charges against the movies have remained essentially the same since the twenties: that they endanger morals, and that they have failed to raise the level of popular taste. In the twenties the movies were violently attacked for their preoccupation with sex, for their lascivious advertising, and for the offscreen escapades of their stars. Under the pressure of public opinion, the industry formed the machinery for self-regulation and drew up the first of its production codes of ethics. Thereafter, critics found fault with the sex and violence in movies, with their distorted picture of American life, and with the juvenility of their plots.

The Department of Justice instituted suits against several of the major film companies in July, 1938, on the grounds that they were engaged in monopolistic practices and in illegal restraint of trade in the production, distribution, and exhibition of motion pictures. After a decade of hearings and litigation, the Supreme Court found that the five fully integrated companies had monopoly of exhibition as a goal, although it did not find monopolistic or illegal practices in production. By 1952, either by court order or consent decree, the five major producers were required to get rid of the theaters they held and to cease certain trade practices held inimical to independent exhibitors.

Criticisms of radio and television have fallen into a familiar pattern, several of them stemming from the domination of programming by two or three major networks. One common complaint has been that programming has rested not with the networks as it should but with the advertiser and his agents, who have prepared the shows, assembled the casts, and bought time to broadcast them, along with their annoying commercials. Another complaint has been that stations have failed to serve their communities by developing local talent, by discussing local issues, and so forth; instead they have become merely outlets for the big networks. Still another common charge has been that the listener has only a fictitious choice of programs; his choice at a given hour is not between culture and comedy but between two comedy shows, both pretty much alike. Critics have spoken out against the heavy balance of entertainment over serious programs and against the low caliber of the entertainment which is offered. In their discussions of public affairs, other critics have charged, radio and television have depended too heavily on conservative commentators and have avoided genuine, healthful controversy. An additional fault has been found with television: Its programming has been heavy on crime and violence.

INTELLECTUAL CLIMATE OF THE NEW THEORY

The intellectual climate of the twentieth century seems to have favored the growth of a theory such as social responsibility and to have blighted libertarian theory. As Alfred North Whitehead once observed, the mentality of an age derives from the world view which is dominant in the educated sections of society, and this world view influences the thought patterns in such areas as ethics, religion, and science (82:viii). A theory of the press which diverges fundamentally from the mentality of its age, then, may well be modified or scrapped altogether. And the libertarian theory is at odds with the emergent world view which seems to be replacing the one which saw its inception, as Jay W. Jensen has plausibly argued (73).

The libertarian theory of the press accommodated itself to the world view of the Enlightenment. Its basis was the perpetual motion world machine of Newton, which ran timelessly according to certain immutable laws of nature; the natural rights philosophy of John Locke with its insistence that freedom was inherent and that man was a rational creature; the doctrines of classical economics with their emphasis on a minimum of governmental interference and their faith that as men worked for their own self-interest they would inevitably work for the common good; and the self-righting process of John Milton, which held that truth would emerge from the free encounter of ideas in the open market.

But the revolution in modern thought has all but demolished the world view which supported the libertarian theory of the press. Shaping the emergent world view of the twentieth century is the Darwin-Einstein revolution, which has wrought profound changes in the thinking of the educated sections of society. Jensen has summed up the impact of modern thought on libertarian theory in this way:

It is clear that the philosophical foundations of the traditional concept of freedom of the press have been precipitously undermined by the revolution in contemporary thought. The static and timeless World-Machine of Newton has been wrecked by the idea of evolution and the dynamic concepts of modern physics. Locke's doctrine of natural rights has been subverted not only by Romantic philosophy but also by present-day social science. Classical *laissez-faire* economics has been repudiated by most contemporary economists, and in practice by almost every modern industrial nation. Moreover, the Miltonian doctrine of the "self-righting process" has lately become suspect (73:405-06).

The ideas which have undermined the Newtonian cosmology and the philosophical underpinnings of traditional theory are in closer harmony with a collectivistic theory of society than with the individualistic theory from which the libertarian system sprang. Each of those two more or less antagonistic theories of society, the individualistic and the collectivistic, has important implications for the functions of the press and, for the way in which the press fulfills them. The individualistic theory presupposes that the individual takes precedence over society; in contrast, the collectivistic theory presupposes that society takes precedence over the individual. At its logical extreme, of course, the collectivistic theory is represented by totalitarianism — by Fascism, by Communism.

However, even a society operating under the principles of individualistic theory does, in some of its aspects, adopt certain elements of the collectivistic. The social responsibility theory of the press represents just such an intermingling of ideas. This is not to say that social responsibility theory even in its extremes indicates a trend toward totalitarianism. On the contrary, the theory poses social responsibility of the media as a safeguard against totalitarianism. The Commission on Freedom of the Press has said that a great potential danger to freedom of the press lies in the appealing notion that the government can solve all of the problems arising from the complexity of modern society and from the concentrations of power; unthinkingly, the nation might move toward totalitarianism if it relies on the government to correct conditions within the press. "If modern society requires great agencies of mass communication, if these concentrations become so powerful that they are a threat to democracy, if democracy cannot solve the problem simply by breaking them up — then those agencies must control themselves or be controlled by government. If they are controlled by government, we lose our chief safeguard against totalitarianism — and at the same time take a long step toward it" (66:5).

The ideas on which democratic capitalism rested also underwent changes in the twentieth century; the belief that each entrepreneur would automatically serve the common good as he selfishly pursued his own interests gave way to the belief that American business and industry must assume certain obligations to the community. The expression "the public be damned" was replaced by the expression "the consumer is king." Alongside this sense of accountability to the public which characterized American business and industry in the twentieth century, the press developed a sense of mission requiring it to serve the general welfare. As it did so, it planted the seeds for a coherent theory of social responsibility.

THE NEW SENSE OF RESPONSIBILITY

Just when the traditional theory of virtually unrestrained freedom began to yield to acceptance by publishers of certain responsibilities, it is hard to say. Certainly publishers were not likely to concern themselves with the ethical aspects of their calling so long as they were primarily printers who regarded their newspapers as adjuncts of their printing establishments, although from the earliest years some journalists had been men of high resolve. By the middle of the nineteenth century, journalism had begun to attract men of education and principle who set high standards for their craft and tried to live up to them. Some such men formulated codes of ethics for their own staffs. The growing professional spirit was no doubt fostered in part by schools of journalism, which began springing up in the first years of this century and which not only taught the techniques of journalism but also in time showed increasing concern with the responsibilities of the media.

As the twentieth century opened, publishers spoke more and more often of the duties which accompanied the privileged position of the press under the constitution. Joseph Pulitzer, defending his proposal for a school of journalism, wrote in the *North American Review* in 1904: "Nothing less than the highest ideals, the most scrupulous anxiety to do right, the most accurate knowledge of the problems it has to meet, and a sincere sense of moral responsibility will save journalism from a subservience to business interests, seeking selfish ends, antagonistic to public welfare" (75:658).

In similar words, as the twentieth century wore on, other publishers spoke not merely of their right to exercise their freedom but also of the responsibilities attached to its exercise. They were joined by moviemakers, by radio and television broadcasters. Publishers in one-newspaper cities spoke of the responsibilities which monopolies imposed upon them. Industry groups formulated codes of ethical performance. And it was not merely the large communications units which spoke thus. Fifty years after Pulitzer had penned his words for the *North American Review,* stockholders of the small *Park Region Echo* at

Alexandria, Minnesota, adopted a declaration of aims which said in part:

To begin with, we must recognize that a truly great newspaper must be greater than any one of, or the combined consciences of its editor in that, when it speaks, its words are those of someone far wiser, far more reasonable, far more fair, far more compassionate, far more understanding and far more honest than those men, crippled by human weaknesses and failings, whose task it is to write those words. . . . A truly great newspaper must remain unfettered by the leash of any and all special interest groups.

The rise of broadcasting made the government a major contributor to the theory of social responsibility. In the early twenties, as radio stations sprouted up in chaotic profusion, competitors broadcast on the same wave lengths, amateurs mixed their signals with those of professionals, and the cacophony was carried into a growing number of listeners' homes. The government, at the urging of the broadcasting industry, reluctantly stepped in to bring some order to the air waves. In 1927 Congress created the Federal Radio Commission to assign frequencies and to keep an eye on program content. The Communications Act of 1934, which reserved radio for operation in the public interest, created the Federal Communications Commission, a permanent agency for issuing broadcast licenses and supervising the air waves.

Although the law expressly forbids F.C.C. censorship of program material, the Commission has taken the position that it is responsible for supervising over-all program content to insure its serving the public interest. While the individual licensee has the right to choose specific program material, the Commission has said, his choice must be "consistent with the basic policy of Congress that radio be maintained as a medium of free speech for the general public as a whole rather than as an outlet for the purely personal or private interests of the licensee" (80:33). The F.C.C.'s policy statements, its actions against some broadcasters and its authority to issue and revoke licenses all have reminded broadcasters that they are trustees, not owners, of the air waves.

Once we have established that both the press and its critics agree that the press should assume responsibilities, we come to a fork in the road. Down one turning goes a theory of social responsibility as it is being evolved by the most articulate spokesmen for the press itself; down the other goes the theory as it has been formulated in its most coherent elaboration by the Commission on Freedom of the Press. Both roads head away from traditional libertarian theory, and they parallel one another for various distances at various places. Although the press was generally hostile to the report of the Commission, its criticisms were not directed to several of the primary assumptions of the report. Evidently few if any of the media took issue with the Commission on the fundamental point that the press has a social responsibility, for example, or even on the function of the press in contemporary democratic society. Indeed, many spokesmen for the press have views coinciding with those of the Commission on those very points, and the Commission has said that it took most of its ideas from the professions of the communications industry itself. What the press did criticize were the Commission's evaluation of press performance, which the press thought was not as bad as the Commission depicted; the Commission's assertion that concentration in the media has endangered the free flow of ideas, to which the press replied that the nature of competition has changed; and, above all, the Commission's suggestion that the power of the government over the media be extended, even cautiously.

Since the writings of the Commission provide the most unified discussion of the goals of social responsibility theory and since those writings have never been analyzed in detail for their implications for traditional theory, most of the balance of this discussion will deal primarily with the social responsibility theory as formulated by the Commission and its member, William Hocking. But let us remember that practitioners, in their professions and practices, contributed a good deal to the shaping of that theory, even if they may not agree with the logical extensions of the Commission's report.

THE CODES REFLECT THE NEW THEORY

And even the codes of ethics of the various media show a changed view of such points as the nature of man and the principles of ethical behavior. The earliest of these codes, the Canons of Journalism, was adopted by the American Society of Newspaper Editors in 1923. It called on newspapers to practice responsibility to the general welfare, sincerity, truthfulness, impartiality, fair play, decency, and respect for the individual's privacy. Perhaps because the newspaper was some three hundred years old when the code was drawn up and hence had a long tradition, the Canons depart less markedly from libertarian theory than do the codes of such twentieth-century media as the movies, radio, and television. Implicit in the Canons are faith that man is primarily a rational creature, able to discover truth and to separate right from wrong by power of reason; faith in the efficacy of the self-righting process; and the belief that the newspaper is chiefly an instrument of enlightenment making its appeal to the critical sense of the reader. The Canons seem to assume that the newspaper should promote democratic government by expediting the self-righting process; the press can aid the workings of the self-righting process by striving for such ideals as truthfulness and fair play. The one new idea in the Canons is that the press is responsible to the general welfare.

The codes of the movie industry in 1930, of the radio industry in 1937 and of the television industry in 1952 reflected the changed intellectual climate. The codes were all drawn up against a background of public hostility to the media. The movie code was formulated to forestall government regulation. The radio and television codes were drawn up by an industry regulated by the government and required to perform in the public interest, convenience, and necessity. The movie code envisions the film as primarily entertainment, although it can contribute to "correct thinking." The radio and television codes regard broadcasting as chiefly a medium of entertainment, although it can serve the economic system by carrying advertising. All three codes see the media as pervasive and as capable of suspending the critical faculties. Perhaps in consequence, the codes reflect a far different picture of man than the newspaper code. All three codes regard man as essentially immature and as highly susceptive to the corruption of his morals. Therefore, ethical performance for those three media differs from that of the newspaper. Ethical behavior as exemplified by the movies code consists of promoting public morals (in general, by promoting marriage and the sanctity of the home and marriage; by respecting religion, law and justice, and national feelings; and by curbing the base emotions). Radio and television codes conceive of ethical behavior as promoting the democratic form of government by enlightening the public, by promoting public morals (in essentially the same way as the movies), and by keeping advertising in good proportion and maintaining high standards for it.

According to the Commission on Freedom of the Press, those codes are not enough to insure the sort of press that society requires. The newspaper code was drawn up by employees, not by employers. Although it would make newspapers responsible carriers of news and discussion if adhered to, the Commission says, it has not been and cannot be enforced. The movie code is merely negative — it sets minimum standards of acceptability, not of responsibility — and its goals are not high enough, according to the Commission. Nor does the broadcasting code have any sanction. The desire to reach the largest possible audience has prevented radio from realizing its potentialities in serving the needs of society.

What does society require from its press? "Its requirements in America today are greater in variety, quantity, and quality than those of any previous society in any age," the Commission says. One reason is the heavy reliance which the American citizen places on the press. He cannot experience much of the world at first-hand, and in an urbanized society he lacks much of the face-to-face discussion which characterized earlier societies. The Kansas farmer who would understand a strike in Detroit, the Detroit automobile worker who would understand the policy of the government regarding atomic energy, the government worker in Washington who would understand the implications of a drought in Kansas — they all must depend upon the mass media. And in ideas as well as in news, Americans must conduct much of their discussion in the press instead of in small face-to-face groups. Yet alongside this growing dependency of Americans on the press in their transactions of public business, ownership of the media has become concentrated into a few hands, and the consumer of news and ideas is largely at the mercy of the operators of the media.

REQUIREMENTS OF PRESS PERFORMANCE

The Commission has listed five things which contemporary society requires of its press, and together they provide a measure of press performance. The standards were not original with the Commission; as the Commission notes, they were drawn largely from the professions and practices of those who operate the media.

The first requirement of the press in contemporary society, according to the Commission, is to provide "a truthful, comprehensive, and intelligent account of the day's events in a context which gives them meaning." This requirement demands that the press be accurate; it must not lie. It means, also, the Commission says, that the press must identify fact as fact and opinion as opinion.

The press itself seems to be in substantial agreement with the Commission that the media should be accurate and should separate news and opinion. There is perhaps no better evidence of this agreement, no better evidence of a growing fidelity to the public interest, than the development of objective reporting, which Herbert Brucker has included among the outstanding achievements of the American newspaper. In the early years of the nineteenth century, papers used the news as a political weapon; it was distorted, biased, and suppressed to meet the needs of the moment. Later in the century newspapers began to confine their opinions to the editorial page; they strove to record the news objectively, without personal intrusion and comment, and to present not just one side but all sides. True, there were economic reasons for the development of objective reporting, apart from a growing sense of professionalism. But there was a philosophical foundation as well. For by separating news and comment, by presenting more than one side, the press was expediting the self-righting process; it was making it easier for the rational reader to discover truth. By the time that the Commission issued its report in 1947, objectivity was no longer a goal of the press; it was a fetish.

But a truthful, comprehensive account of the news is not enough, says the Commission. "It is no longer enough to report the *fact* truthfully. It is now necessary to report *the truth about the fact.*" Here then is the suggestion that the press has developed a curious sort of objectivity — a spurious objectivity which results in half-truths, incompleteness, incomprehensibility. In adhering to objective reporting, the press has tried to present more than one side to a story; but in doing so, the suggestion is, the media have not bothered to evaluate for the reader the trustworthiness of conflicting sources, nor have they supplied the perspective essential to a complete understanding of a given situation. Instead of assuming that two half-truths make a truth, the Commission says in effect, the press should seek "the whole truth."

On this point, too, the press seems to agree with the Commission, although less wholeheartedly than with the assertion that the media should publish the truth and should separate fact and opinion. Indeed, it is because of its fidelity to the public interest that the press has been reluctant, as the Commission puts it, to publish the truth about the fact. Putting into the one-dimensional story the other dimensions which will make it approximate the truth entails serious dangers, according to Elmer Davis, the radio commentator, who has expressed the dilemma of the press in this fashion:

I have seen some undeniably well-intentioned endeavors to put in those other dimensions, but the dimensions were derived not from the evidence but from the opinions or prejudices of the reporter; and if the practice were to become general they might in some cases be derived from the opinions and prejudices of the publisher, as they so often used to be. One Chicago *Tribune* is enough. And even if a man's conscience is as rigorous, his mind as relentlessly objective, as the weights and measures in the Bureau of Standards, he may still fall short of doing as accurate a job as he means to do because he doesn't know all the angles, or hasn't time to get around to them under the pressure of covering what is in front of him and writing a story about it (67:173-74).

But despite the dilemma, Davis concludes, the press should do a better job of trying to put the news into proper context.

The good newspaper, the good news broadcaster, must walk a tightrope between two great gulfs — on one side the false objectivity that takes everything at face value and lets the public be imposed upon by the charlatan with the most brazen front; on the other, the "interpretive" reporting which fails to draw the line between objective and subjective, between a reasonably well-established fact and what the reporter or editor wishes were fact. To say that is easy; to do it is hard (67:175).

The nine newspapermen who attended Harvard as Nieman Fellows in 1945-46 also support the Commission in its plea for the truth about the facts. Like Davis, the Nieman Fellows acknowledge that "truth" is elusive and that the pressures of producing a daily newspaper make it difficult for a reporter to get all the facts requisite for a multidimensioned treatment of the news. "Yet," they concluded, "there are dozens of disputes in each day's paper concerning which some approximations to truth can be asserted." If Senator Byrd says that a million government employees can be dismissed without impairing the efficiency of the government, if the President says "Nonsense," who is right? "Clearly it must be the function of the press in a democracy to answer such questions," the Nieman Fellows say, "and to answer them honestly" (79:27). The increase of interpretation in the daily press in the past two decades and the attempts by such broadcasters as Edward R. Murrow to put the news in context suggest that a growing number of practitioners are subscribing to the view that merely reporting the news is insufficient.

A second requirement of the press, according to the Commission, is that it serve as "a forum for the exchange of comment and criticism." This requirement means that the great agencies of mass communications should regard themselves as common carriers of public discussion, although it does not mean that laws should compel them to accept all applicants for space or that the government should regulate their rates or even that one can demand, as a right, that the media disseminate his ideas. In simple terms, it means that the giants of the press should carry views contrary to their own without abdicating their own right of advocacy. The press should try to represent all important viewpoints, not merely those with which the publisher or operator agrees; and in doing so, it should carefully identify all sources of news. The reason for this requirement is that control of the press has become vested in fewer and fewer hands. No longer can the individual with something to say reach the necessary audience with the unaided human voice, no longer can he found a newspaper or magazine, no longer can he issue his ideas in pamphlets which will have the prestige that the mass media confer upon their contents.

On this point, too, the media operators seem to concur in large measure with the Commission. Thus Norman Isaacs, managing editor of the Louisville *Times* and 1952-53 president of the Associated Press Managing Editors Association, has stated: "The one function we have that supersedes everything is to convey information. We are common carriers. The freedom of the press was given for that purpose — and that purpose alone. Freedom of the press cannot mean the license to keep people from knowing. And we keep them from knowing whenever we are backward and arrogant in operating our papers" (72:15). Editors and publishers are fond of saying that the growth of one-newspaper cities has been accompanied by an increased sense of duty to their communities among the dailies which have survived. Spokesmen for the Cowles newspapers in Des Moines and Minneapolis have said that the one daily in a city has a greater responsibility than ever to "help society inform itself and act intelligently" and that the editorial page is an important medium for supplementing and complementing the reporting of news. In both editorial content and advertising, the monopolistic trend in the newspaper field has put new responsibilities on publishers, according to Edward Lindsay of the Lindsay-Schaub Newspapers. "They have a responsibility to minorities in the publication of complete and objective news accounts," he wrote in one of his papers. "They have a responsibility at the business level. Newspaper publishers are denied the luxury of refusing to deal with those whom they dislike or of using their control of a medium of communication to punish those who patronize a competitor. . . ."

In their code, broadcasters speak of exerting every effort to insure equality of opportunity in the discussion of public issues; and the television code advises stations to "give fair representation to opposing sides of issues which materially affect the life or welfare of a substantial segment of the public."

A third requirement of the press, the Commission states, is that it project "a representative picture of the constituent groups in society." Closely related to the preceding two, this requirement would have the press accurately portray the social groups, the Chinese and the Negroes, for example, since persons tend to make decisions in terms of favorable or unfavorable images and a false picture can subvert accurate judgment. In principle if not in practice, most media operators would perhaps concur with the Commission. The movie, radio, and television codes all contain statements urging the media to respect national feelings and the sensitivity of racial and religious groups. Newspaper and magazine workers probably would say that this requirement is implicit in their conscientious effort to report the day's intelligence truthfully and impartially.

A fourth requirement mentioned by the Commission is that the press be responsible for "the presentation and clarification of the goals and values of the society." Again, practitioners would probably accept this requirement with little hesitation. Newsmen would perhaps respond, for instance, that one function of a good editorial page is just such presentation and clarification. Movie producers and broadcasters could point to their codes of performance, which urge the media to respect accepted values and to portray the traditional virtues.

The final requirement mentioned by the Commission is that the press provide "full access to the day's intelligence." Since the citizen today requires more current information than in any earlier day, the Commission notes, there must be a wide distribution of news and opinion. The press would certainly agree. Apart from the attempts of the press to reach as wide an audience as possible, there is evidence of the agreement, for example, in the evolution of the concept of "freedom of information." As newsmen became imbued with a sense of responsibility, they contended that the public had a right of access to information, had a basic right to be informed, and that the press was the agent of the public in breaking down barriers to the free flow of news.

The idea marked a break with traditional theory, which assured the citizen access to the day's intelligence only by protecting freedom of expression. Traditional theory provided no legal tool for prying open the lips of the silent. Yet during World War II and after, especially, newspapermen complained of an increasing number of government officials at local, state, and national levels who refused to release information which might embarrass certain officeholders. Championing the public's right to such information, the American Society of Newspaper Editors and other professional groups formed committees to help open up the sources of news; and such newsmen as James Reston, James Pope, and Erwin Canham repeatedly warned of the dangers of censorship by suppression.

WAYS OF IMPROVING PRESS PERFORMANCE

Those, then, are the standards of performance outlined by the Commission. Although the press itself seems to accept those standards, the Commission detects a wide breach between the acknowledgment of those standards by the press and its actual practice. For improvement in press performance, the Commission looks to three sources — to the press itself, to the public, and to the government.

The press, to provide the variety, quantity, and quality of information and discussion which the public requires, the Commission says, should assume a professional spirit. "Whatever may be thought of the conduct of individual members of the older, established professions, like law and medicine," it notes, "each of these professions as a whole accepts a responsibility for the service rendered by the profession as a whole, and there are some things which a truly professional man will not do for money" (66:92). Specifically, the press should assume the responsibilities of common carriers of information and discussion, should experiment with high quality content which offers no immediate promise of financial return, should engage in vigorous mutual criticism, and should seek to improve the caliber of its personnel. The radio industry should take control of programming away from advertisers.

But the public too has certain obligations toward the press. What is needed first is a public awareness of the tremendous power enjoyed by the mass media, power concentrated in too few hands; an awareness of how far the press fails to meet the needs of society. Once the public understands those things, it can act in three ways to improve the press. First, nonprofit institutions should help the press carry out its required tasks. For example, colleges might operate radio stations or produce movies for audiences which the commercial media find it inexpedient to serve. Second, educational institutions should create centers for advanced study, research, and critical publication in the field of mass communications; the present schools of journalism should give students the broadest of educations. Third, an independent agency should be established to appraise press performance and to report on it each year.

The government, recognizing that the press must remain a privately-owned business, can nevertheless help to give its citizens the kind of communications system that they require. For instance, the government can encourage new ventures in the communications industry. It can adopt new legal remedies to rectify chronic, patent abuses of press freedom. And it can enter the communications field to supplement the privately-owned media.

NEGATIVE AND POSITIVE FREEDOM

The social responsibility theory of the press rests on a foundation of thought which has amended certain fundamental assumptions of libertarian theory and which has largely rejected others. The concept of liberty which it represents is fundamentally different from that which traditional theory represented. Libertarian theory was born of a concept of negative liberty, which we can define loosely as "freedom from" and more precisely as "freedom from external restraint." The social responsibility theory, on the contrary, rests on a concept of positive liberty, "freedom for," which calls for the presence of the necessary implements for the attainment of a desired goal. Let us explore this point more fully.

In sum, negative liberty consisted of leaving the individual free to work out his own destiny. If he were free from outside forces, he could do so by using his reason to discover the unchanging laws of nature which governed the universe and by bringing his institutions into harmony with them. It was enough, then, to remove the restrictions on man. And it was enough to remove all but a minimum of restrictions on the press; for if the press were unhampered, it would feed information and ideas into the market place, and from their interchange truth would emerge triumphant.

The social responsibility theory is grounded in a school of thought which sees a purely negative liberty as insufficient and ineffective. Negative liberty, according to this view, is an empty liberty; it is like telling a man that he is free to walk without first making sure that he is not crippled. To be real, freedom must be effective. It is not enough to tell a man that he is free to achieve his goals; one must provide him with the appropriate means of attaining those goals.

Hocking, whose ideas are clearly discernible in the report of the Commission as a whole, has said that true freedom must have both its negative and positive aspects. "To be free," he says, "is to have the use of one's powers of action (i) without restraint or control from outside and (ii) with whatever means or equipment the action requires" (69:54).

The Commission also says that effective freedom has its positive as well as negative aspects. "As with all freedom," it says, "press freedom means freedom from and freedom for." A free press is free *from* all compulsions, although not from all pressures. It is free *for* achieving the goals defined by its ethical sense and by society's needs; and to attain this end, it must have technical facilities, financial strength, access to information, and so forth (66:128). But the Commission is concerned not just about freedom of those who own the media; it is also concerned about citizens who possess a merely negative freedom of expression. Freedom of the press, the Commission argues, is a somewhat empty right for the person who lacks access to the mass media. His freedom, too, must be implemented — by a press which carries viewpoints similar to his own; by media operated by government or nonprofit agencies to provide him with the required services which the commercial press does not provide.

Even the press itself has been edging away from a concept of negative liberty as a result of its preoccupation with "freedom of information." The press found that a system of negative liberty provided no instruments for prying information from recalcitrant government officials. In various states, the press has worked for the passage of laws which would require certain official bodies to transact their business in open meetings and to make their records available for scrutiny by the press.

THE PRESS AND GOVERNMENT

As one might expect, the social responsibility theory also differs from traditional theory in the view which it takes of the nature and functions of government. Libertarian theory evolved during a period in which the state was regarded as the chief foe of liberty. True, there were other threats to it; John Stuart Mill recognized that the tyranny of the majority, as surely as the hand of the state, could infringe upon an individual's freedom. Yet by and large, freedom came to mean freedom from the hold of the state, and the best form of government came to be taken as that which governed least. Some government was necessary to maintain internal and external security — to preserve civil order, for instance, and to ward off aggressors — and thus to provide a climate in which freedom could exist. But the object of concern was freedom of the individual. If one assured the freedom of the individual, then one assured the freedom of society.

Social responsibility theory holds that the government must not merely allow freedom; it must also actively promote it. As under traditional theory, one function of government is to maintain order and personal security. But that is essentially a negative function which leaves the exercise of freedom to chance, and it is not sufficient in modern societies. Along with the community, the government, with its virtual monopoly on physical force, is the only agency strong enough to make sure that freedom can operate effectively. When necessary, therefore, the government should act to protect the freedom of its citizens.

"Government remains the residuary legatee of responsibility for an adequate press performance," says Hocking, and his opinion seems shared by the Commission as a whole. The government should help society to obtain the services it requires from the mass media if a self-regulated press and the self-righting features of community life are insufficient to provide them. The government may act in several ways. It may enact legislation to forbid flagrant abuses of the press which "poison the wells of public opinion," for example, or it may enter the field of communication to supplement existing media (69:182-93).

Even so, the press must still have a foundation in private enterprise. The government should intervene only when the need is great and the stakes are high, and then it should intervene cautiously. It should not aim at competing with or eliminating privately-owned media.

In short, the government should not act with a heavy hand. Any agency capable of promoting freedom is also capable of destroying it. Since freedom of expression is the keystone of political liberty, it must be especially protected. Even a democratic government can infringe the freedom of its citizens. Public officials, whose tenure in office depends in large measure on public opinion, may be tempted to control expression. Therefore,

If the freedom of the press is to achieve reality, government must set limits on its capacity to interfere with, regulate, or suppress the voices of the press or to manipulate the data on which public judgment is formed.

Government must set the limits on itself, not merely because freedom of expression is a reflection of important interests of the community, but also because it is a moral right. It is a moral right because it has an aspect of duty about it (66:8).

THE RIGHT OF EXPRESSION

Freedom of expression is a moral right with an aspect of duty about it, according to the social responsibility theory. The theory thus differs from libertarian theory on the nature of the right. For under libertarian theory, freedom of expression was a natural right, a right which man was born with, a right which no one could take away, although its exercise might temporarily be prevented. No duty was attached to the right. As we have seen, the assumption was that free men would voice their ideas and that other free men would listen. Men with ideas were not obligated to speak, others were not obligated to listen; but given the nature of man, it was inconceivable that they would not. While free expression was a natural right, it also was grounded on utility. It was justified because free speech and a free press would promote the victory of truth over falsehood in the market place of ideas.

Under social responsibility theory, freedom of expression is grounded on the duty of the individual to his thought, to his conscience. It is a moral right; and a moral right, in the words of Hocking, is "a value which I am not free to relinquish, as I am free to relinquish a personal interest." If one claims free expression as a right, he claims it for others as well as himself and he binds himself to respect their exercise of it; if he yields his claim, he weakens the claim of others (69:60-61). Freedom of expression is not something which one claims for selfish ends. It is so closely bound up with his mental existence and growth that he *ought* to claim it. It has value both for the individual and for society. It is the individual's means of perpetuating himself through his ideas. It is society's sole source of intelligence, the seeds from which progress springs.

Besides being valuable to the individual and to society, free expression has an aspect of duty about it, for anyone with something to say is morally bound to say it. "If a man is burdened with an idea," says the Commission, "he not only desires to express it; he ought to express it. He owes it to his conscience and the common good. The indispensable function of expressing ideas is one of obligation — to the community and also to something beyond the community — let us say to truth. It is the duty of the scientist to his results and of Socrates to his oracle; it is the duty of every man to his own belief. Because of this duty to what is beyond the state, freedom of speech and of the press are moral rights which the state must not infringe" (66:8-9).

This duty to one's conscience is the primary basis of the right of free expression under social responsibility theory. It is a basis which the Commission sees as logically preceding the traditional justification of free expression on the grounds of utility. For whatever discussion arises from free expression is the result of this duty of the individual to his conscience.

Although free expression is a universal right, the citizen cannot claim the right to reach the audience of any of the mass media. He cannot demand, as a right, that a newspaper or radio station transmit what he says.

Freedom of expression under the social responsibility theory is not an absolute right, as under pure libertarian theory. "The notion of rights, costless, unconditional, conferred by the Creator at birth, was a marvelous fighting principle against arbitrary governments and had its historical work to do," says the Commission. "But in the context of an achieved political freedom the need of limitation becomes evident" (66:121). One's right to free expression must be balanced against the private rights of others and against vital social interests.

On this score, traditional theory had been modified long before the Commission on Freedom of the Press came along. In 1919, in the case of *Schenck vs. the United States,* Justice Holmes formulated the "clear and present danger" test for determining when free expression may be abridged. "The question in every case," he wrote, "is whether the words used are used in such circumstances and are of such a nature as to create a clear and present danger that they will bring about the substantive evils that Congress has a right to prevent. It is a question of proximity and degree." The press itself acknowledged that considerations of public welfare could override its right to free utterance, as when it submitted to voluntary censorship in both of the world wars.

The conditional nature of free expression, in the Commission's line of reasoning, arises from the basis of the right. Free expression is grounded on man's duty to his thought. If man does not assume this duty to his conscience, if on the contrary he uses his free expression to inflame hatred, to vilify, to lie, if he uses it deliberately to contaminate the springs of truth, then he has no claim to the right. He has a moral right only if he assumes the concomitant moral duty.

The moral right to free expression does carry with it the right to be in error. There are at least two good reasons for tolerating error. One is that social responsibility theory, like the libertarian theory, assumes that the search for truth and the spread of truth require considerable freedom. As the Commission puts it, "liberty is experimental, and experiment implies trial and error." A second reason is that each individual has the right to be sure that he has found truth through his own free discovery instead of having it imposed upon him by some authority. But the moral right covers only honest error. Even the individual who is wrong must be conscientiously seeking truth. One does not have the right to be deliberately or irresponsibly in error.

In linking rights and duties, social responsibility theory bears a closer resemblance to Soviet theory than to libertarian. Soviet theory, like social responsibility theory, predicates the exercise of rights on the acceptance of accompanying duties. But there is a profound difference between the two theories. Under Soviet theory, the duty is to the proletariat; under the social responsibility theory, the duty is to one's own conscience.

Moreover, in Soviet theory, one forfeits his legal claim to the right of free expression if he ignores the duty on which it depends. Not so in social responsibility theory. Even if one sacrifices his moral right to free expression he may still claim a legal right to it. The law is not a fine enough instrument to measure how closely the individual serves his conscience. It must assume that men in general are speaking in good faith and in an earnest quest for truth. It is questionable that the law should make free expression responsible even if it could. For many individuals, lying is an experiment in morality, as Hocking has noted, and society has some correctives against it. It is far more in keeping with a free society that men achieve responsibility through their own volition and self-control than through some external force.

Therefore, the law must protect some persons who do not assume their moral responsibilities along with all of those who do.

But the legal right to free expression under the social responsibility theory is not unconditional. Even libertarian theory imposed certain minimal restraints on free expression such as laws dealing with libel, obscenity, incitement to riot, and sedition. All of those restrictions, the Commission has noted, were based on one common principle: "that an utterance or publication invades in a serious, overt, and demonstrable manner recognized private rights or vital social interests" (66:123). The legal restrictions on press freedom, then, it argued, might be justifiably extended if new abuses fall within this category.

Take for example degradation. If publications deliberately, consistently, systematically pander in and exploit vulgarity, they have sacrificed their moral right to free expression. Having abandoned their moral claim to it, they have undermined their legal claim. True, there might be a better means than the law of correcting such publications. Yet society may decide that degradation is an invasion of its vital interests against which it is justified in protecting itself. Therefore, it might prohibit degrading publications. However, the burden of proof that society's interests were harmed would rest with whoever would extend the law to cover such new areas of abuse.

VIEW OF THE NATURE OF MAN

The social responsibility theory seems to differ fundamentally from libertarian theory in its view of the nature of man. Under traditional theory, man was regarded as primarily a moral and rational being who was inclined to hunt for truth and to be guided by it. Every man by nature wished to aid the quest for truth, and every man could serve its cause, for even the most seemingly preposterous idea was worth expression. Only if all men spoke freely what was on their minds, the ridiculous as well as the sublime, could they hope to discover truth. Given freedom to speak and to publish, men would express themselves. They would do so temperately and without capriciousness. There was no need to remind publishers of their public responsibilities; they would assume them without exhortation because of the moral sense which gave them their dignity. Nor need one worry about the occasional publisher who, because of human frailty, lied or distorted. Other publishers would find it profitable to expose him. His lies and distortions would be recognized, for the public would put his utterances to the powerful test of reason.

The social responsibility theory, on the other hand, was developed in the twentieth century, and it reflects the doubts which contemporary social science and contemporary thought have cast on the rationality of man. The emerging theory does not deny the rationality of man, although it puts far less confidence in it than libertarian theory, but it does seem to deny that man is innately motivated to search for truth and to accept it as his guide. Under the social responsibility theory, man is viewed not so much irrational as lethargic. He is capable of using his reason, but he is loath to do so. Consequently, he is easy prey for demagogues, advertising pitchmen, and others who would manipulate him for their selfish ends. Because of his mental sloth, man has fallen into a state of unthinking conformity, to which his inertia binds him. His mental faculties have become stultified and are in danger of atrophy. If man is to remain free, he must live by reason instead of passively accepting what he sees, hears, and feels. Therefore, the more alert elements of the community must goad him into the exercise of his reason. Without such goading, man is not likely to be moved to seek truth. The languor which keeps him from using his gift of reason extends to all public discussion. Man's aim is not to find truth but to satisfy his immediate needs and desires.

The skeptical view of man is even more pronounced in the media codes except the Canons of Journalism than in the writings of the Commission. The codes of the movie and broadcasting industries regard safeguarding public morals as a chief concern of the media. They do not in the least reflect the Miltonian ideas that man through reason can distinguish between right and wrong, that he cannot be regarded as truly moral unless he has been subjected to temptation, and that he is better off learning of evil through the media than at first hand.

The Commission puts a greater faith in man's morality than do those codes. Indeed, on the surface the Commission seems to share the faith that traditional theory placed in man's morality. But morality to the Commission appears to be a different thing than morality under libertarian theory. Traditional theory was based on the assumption that man, as a child of God or of some creator, was an autonomous creature of dignity who adhered to certain absolute principles of ethical behavior. To express it loosely, he was true to himself; and because he was true to himself, he was true to his fellow man. Morality under social responsibility theory seems more relative than under libertarian theory. Nor is it primarily duty to self. As a social being, man owes a duty to his fellow beings; and morality is duty not primarily to oneself but to the interests of the community.

The moral duties which were implicit in libertarian theory become explicit in social responsibility theory. The citizen, under libertarian theory, had the right to be uninformed or misinformed, but the tacit assumption was that his rationality and his desire for truth would keep him from being so. The Commission specifically states that the citizen is no longer morally free not to read, not to listen. As an active and responsible citizen, one has a duty to the community to be informed. This is not to say that one must read or listen to any given segment or product of the press. Like traditional theory, the new one recognizes that the citizen's approval or disapproval is an effective control on the media. The citizen is morally obligated to be informed; how he becomes so is his own choice.

If a man has a moral duty to be informed, the Commission says, one can logically hold that he has a right to information for carrying out that duty. Hence it is no longer sufficient merely to protect the press's right of free expression, as under traditional theory; it also is imperative to protect the citizen's right to adequate information.

A press characterized by bigness, fewness, and costliness in effect holds freedom of the press in trust for the entire population. Media operators and owners are denied the right of publishing what pleases themselves. Free expression being a moral right, they are obligated to make sure that all significant viewpoints of the citizenry are represented in the press. They need not publish every idea, however preposterous, of course; but they should see that "all ideas deserving a public hearing shall have a public hearing." The public as well as the editors and owners should decide what ideas deserve a public hearing (66:119).

But the Commission thinks it questionable that press performance can be left to unregulated initiative alone. The citizen has a moral right to information and an urgent need for it. If the press does not of its volition fill his requirements, then both the community and the government should protect his interests. They can do so by taking the measures mentioned earlier in this discussion.

THE SELF-RIGHTING PROCESS

Social responsibility theory puts far less faith than libertarian theory in the efficacy of the self-righting process. Milton would have subjected all but primary assumptions to the test of free debate, and Mill and Jefferson would have exempted not even first principles. Their conviction that truth will rise majestically from the clash of ideas is scarcely justified in contemporary society, according to shapers of social responsibility theory. Hocking asks, "If one makes it a principle to commit all principles to the melting-pot of debate, what becomes of the principles which decide debate, what way has he of emerging from an endlessly renewed clash of hypotheses?" (69:15). In short, debate becomes inconclusive; there is no one, as Hocking observes, to pronounce victory or defeat.

Furthermore, Hocking continues, actualities do not support the classical position. First, there is no assurance that idea will clash against idea in any real contest. Second, few citizens genuinely search for ideas which attack those they already hold. "What the existing process does achieve," says Hocking, "is to elicit mental power and breadth in those participants whom it does not baffle or confuse. As long as the will to find truth is undiscouraged and lively, free expression tends to produce a stronger and more self-conscious citizenry. It is less its truth product than its human product which we can count on" (69:94-95).

One can only speculate on what the Commission regards to be the nature of truth, for the word "truth" seldom enters into its discussion. One gathers that the Commission does not regard the chief aim of free expression to be the discovery of an absolute truth, as it was under libertarian theory. Free expression was valued under traditional theory because it led to the revelation of truth. To the shapers of that theory, of course, truth meant different things at different times. To Milton, truth was the will of a Puritan God; to Jefferson, it probably was an understanding of the marvelous plan under which the universe operated. It was an absolute to both, capable of discovery through the free interchange of ideas.

The Commission appears to value free expression chiefly because it promotes the harmonious, fruitful society. Man, free to express himself, free to exchange ideas with his neighbors, grows in dignity and develops to his fullest capabilities, as Mill suggested. If free expression does not lead to the discovery of an absolute truth, it can at least lead to the discovery of a number of lesser truths, tentative truths, working truths, which enable men to lead rich and peaceful lives. The value of free expression is that it raises social conflict "from the plane of violence," as the Commission expresses it, "to the plane of discussion" (66:113).

That, then, is the social responsibility theory as developed by the Commission on Freedom of the Press. The reports of the Commission have been called "unrealistic." In some of their specific recommendations, they well may be. Yet one significant point seems to have been generally overlooked. The Commission has accepted the communications revolution and complex twentieth-century life and has tried to solve the problems of the press within that context. Furthermore, its recommendations in large measure accommodate themselves to the emergent world view and the thought patterns resulting from it. In one sense, therefore, few other critics have been so realistic; most critics, like Morris Ernst in his *The First Freedom* (New York: Macmillan, 1946), have sought to recapture the happy ideal of the eighteenth and nineteenth centuries in a twentieth-century milieu. This point may be comforting if one agrees with the Commission or disturbing if one does not.

Whether or not one agrees with the Commission, however, one conclusion is abundantly evident — pure libertarian theory is obsolescent, as the press as a whole has in fact recognized. Taking its place is an emerging theory which puts increasing emphasis on the responsibilities of the press, although it is still too early to discern what the full-blown form of the theory will be. Individuals who still speak of freedom of the press as a purely personal right are a diminishing breed, lonely and anachronistic.

THE SOVIET COMMUNIST

THEORY OF

THE PRESS

WILBUR SCHRAMM 4

On the rare occasions when United States and Soviet newspapermen come together to discuss mass communication, the talk is apt to be both amusing and frustrating; for it becomes obvious in the first few minutes that the two frames of reference are incompatible. The American feels blessed with his free press, and is inclined to sympathize with his Soviet colleague who groans under state ownership, censorship, and propaganda. The Soviet representative, on the other hand, claims that *he* is blessed with the only true freedom of the press, whereas his unfortunate American colleague is compelled to serve a press that is venal, controlled by special interests, corrupt, and irresponsible. The American speaks proudly of the ability of his press and wire services to bring him late news from all over the world, and the ability of his mass media to entertain and amuse him. The Soviet man expresses the opinion that late news is not a very important public service, and that most of the entertainment in the American media is "twaddle," unworthy of a great nation. And so it goes, until each backs off — suspecting the other of being addled.

The purpose of this paper is to try to bridge the bewildering gap between these two points of view. In order to understand the present Soviet theory of mass communication, we shall try to trace it from its roots in Marx through its mutations in the gardens of Lenin and Stalin. We shall examine the present theory in some detail and look at the communication system which has grown out of it. Finally, we shall try to relate the Soviet theory to other theories that have grown up in other parts of the world, including our own. And let us begin where the Soviet idea began, with Karl Marx.

1. BACKGROUND

THE MARXIST BASIS

"What was social science before Marx?" asked Andrei Vyshinsky, and answered his own question thus:

"Pre-Marxian sociology" and historiography at best presented a desultory assemblage of crude facts and a portrayal of separate sides of the historic process. Marxism pointed the way to an all-embracing, omnifarious study of the process of emergence, development, and decay of social-economic formations. It contemplates the totality of all contradictory tendencies and reduces them to precisely defined conditions of the life and production of the various classes of society. It eliminates subjectivism and arbitrariness in choosing or interpreting "master" ideas. It exposes, without exception, the roots of all ideas and all different tendencies in the condition of material production forces (116:82).

It seems almost as though Mr. Vyshinsky did protest too much. Marx himself more than once expressed dissatisfaction with what his followers were doing to his ideas. "Je ne suis pas Marxiste," he said in disgust, and he might make another such disclaimer today if he could see what has happened to his doctrine in Russia and the other Communist countries. For the tradition of Marx has undergone profound changes both in the hands of later custodians of the word and under the pressure of events and situations which could not have been foreseen when Marx wrote.

Nevertheless, it is clear that Marx contributed a general outlook and at least three sets of ideas which have been the foundation stones for everything his Soviet followers have built.

The outlook is not easy to state in a few words, and yet it is suggested in the passage we have just quoted from Vyshinsky: Marxism tries to be "all-embracing"; it "contemplates . . . totality"; it "eliminates subjectivism . . . in choosing . . . ideas"; it tries to reveal common roots of "all ideas and all different tendencies." In other words, Marxism is a *general* philosophy of history, and it has the overtones of doctrine. It is a neater, tighter system than democracy. Democracy from the beginning has defended the rights of men to disagree — with each other, with their government, with religions. Democracy has developed in such a path that free men are often unable to agree on common objectives, or even on the amount of freedom men should have. Marx and his followers, on the other hand, have placed an almost mystical value on "unity" — unity of the working class, unity of the Party, unity of choice amongst alternatives. "How could one of your elections possibly be free if the wrong side won?" a Russian once asked me, and in so saying he was explaining more clearly than we could possibly explain by pages of analysis just what this Marxist outlook is. From the beginning, the Marxist tradition has displayed authoritarianism, fixedness, a tendency to make hard and sharp distinction between right and wrong, an amazing confidence in explaining great areas of human behavior on the basis of a small set of economic facts.

This inheritance from Marx takes on its true importance in the hands of the Russian people, of whom Carlyle used to say that their pre-eminent talent was the talent to obey, and who have become used to authority through centuries of experiencing it. The ideal of unity and generality derived from Marx is clearly related to the Soviet policy of repression, the Communist habit of ignoring or explaining away conflicting evidence, and the missionary-like zeal of many Communist agitators. And in this general outlook inherited by Russians from Marx we have the basis of much misunderstanding between the Soviet Union and the United States. We are apt to think that people must and should hold different ideas and values, and therefore to encourage the arts of compromise and majority rule; the Soviet Russians are apt to think that men should *not* hold different viewpoints, that compromise is a sign of weakness, that there is one *right* position to be found in Marxism interpretation and to be defended, propagated, and enforced. To us, what Muller calls the "famed Russian unity" (105:310) seems reactionary and tyrannical. To the Russians, our lack of agreement, our permissiveness toward argument, compromise, and criticism, seem anarchy or chaos.

In the shadow of this general attitude, Marx developed his concept of social change which we can describe in terms of its dynamics (the dialectic), its motivation (materialistic determinism), and its goal (victory of the working class and ultimately a classless, stateless society).

The dialectic of social change

The relation of change to the changeless has always been a central preoccupation of philosophers. The general trend — represented by most of the great philosophers of Asia, and western philosophers in the Platonist and Christian traditions — has been to concern oneself chiefly with contemplating the changeless. But Marx, it must be remembered, grew up in a century and in a part of the world where change was studied and dramatically exemplified. His century was the time of evolutionary theory in biology, and of dramatic social change resulting from the industrial revolution. He gloried in change, studied the process, tried, as Brinton says, "to find in change itself the answer to the riddle of change" (85:204).

He found his answer chiefly in Hegel's concept of the *dialectic* by which two opposing forces *(thesis* and *antithesis)* resolve their differences in a *synthesis.* This synthesis in turn becomes a thesis which is opposed by a new antithesis, from which grows a new synthesis — and so on through history. Marx used this dialectic to interpret history as a succession of class struggles. For example, the struggle of the feudal, manorial class (thesis) with the new bourgeois class of merchants, capitalists, and manufacturers (antithesis), began in the Renaissance and culminated in the American and French Revolutions of the eighteenth century which were complete victories for the new bourgeoisie (synthesis).

Marx felt, however, that these were not true revolutions and the result was not a true social synthesis, because they were *political* rather than social revolutions; the result was a change of ruling power rather than any profound social change. This latter, he thought, would come from the opposition of the working class (antithesis) to the bourgeoisie (thesis), with the result being victory for the workers and the formation of a new classless society (synthesis). Whether the process of dialectical change would stop with this classless society, he does not make clear. More important, however, is the difference between Marx's and Hegel's viewpoints toward the nature of this dialectic.

The basis in materialistic determinism

Marx said:

My dialectic method is not only different from the Hegelian, but is its direct opposite. To Hegel, the life-process of the human brain, i.e., the process of thinking, which, under the name of "the Idea," he even transforms into an independent subject, is the demiurgos of the real world, and the real world is only the external, phenomenal form of "the Idea." With me, on the contrary, the idea is nothing else than the material world reflected by the human mind, and translated into forms of thought. . . . With him (Hegel) it (dialectics) is standing on its head. It must be turned right side up again, if you would discover the rational kernel within the mystical shell (103:25).

Marx's great contribution was to turn Hegel's dialectic "on its head." He made it realistic, instead of idealistic. He argued that the material conditions of life — chiefly man's way of making his living and the kind of living he makes — determine man's ideas. In other words, economics, the system of productive forces and productive relations, is the central factor of the life of man, the fact which, as George Kennan put it, determines the nature of a public life and the physiognomy of society.

Reflecting on this determinism and studying the economics of western Europe, Marx arrived at a paradigm for social change which he felt was inevitable. He believed that productive forces would always change faster than productive relations, thus throwing society out of balance. As he analyzed the situation, capitalism contained the seeds of its own destruction. It would always have recurring depressions and economic crises. These would broaden the gulf between rich and poor. The rich would grow richer and the poor poorer. But the rich would grow fewer and the poor more numerous and more desperate. The last stage of capitalism would be imperialism, which would breed wars and more misery. Finally, the working class would no longer be able to contain their frustration. They would rise and take over the means of production, liquidate the capitalists, and organize a new classless society.

He makes plain that this change is much more than economic or political. The arts, religion, philosophy, and all other components of culture would likewise change. For his position is, as Jensen and others point out, that inevitably the dominant ideas and institutions of any society are the ideas and institutions of the dominant economic class.

The goal: a classless, stateless society

Now let us look for a moment at the goal and end of all this social change. When the proletariat takes over the means of production, said Engels, when it "puts an end to itself as the proletariat, it puts an end to class differences and class antagonisms, it puts an end also to the state as state. . . . The first act in which the state really comes forward as the representative of society as a whole — the seizure of the means of production in the name of society — is, at the same time, its last independent act as a state" (89:410). From that moment on, the state must "automatically wither away." The state, as Marx and Engels see it, is merely a device for one class to exercise control over others. With a classless society, therefore, the state is by definition obsolete.

What an extraordinarily optimistic view of man this is! Not even a fiery champion of democracy like Thomas Paine ever thought man so nearly perfect that he could live without government! But there is a flaw in the picture. Is man ready at once to play his appointed part in this golden age? Marx indicated that he is not, for he must accept the leadership, even the dictatorship, of the Party. What is the process, then, by which man is educated to his position "just below the angels" and the state is enabled to wither away? Once man has been organized into "a machine to change society," as Stephen Spender puts it (97), how shall he be turned into the godlike free creature Marx apparently envisages? On this point, both Marx and Engels have very little to say. They insist on the inevitability of the golden age, but are not very specific about how it will be arrived at once power has been seized. As we shall see later, their followers have also had some trouble with the details of the golden age. Indeed, the fact that the Soviet state has thus far shown no sign of withering away, and instead has vastly multiplied its bureaucracy and its police system, has caused some embarrassment to Communist apologists.

Although Marx almost never addressed himself to the problem of mass communication, still the basis for the Soviet rationale is in what we have been talking about. For one thing, it is clear that the Marxist concept of unity and the sharp distinction between right and wrong positions, would not permit the press to function as a Fourth Estate, independently criticizing government or serving as a forum for free discussion. Rather, the Communist press would be conceived as an instrument to interpret the doctrine, to carry out the policies of the working class or the militant party. Again, it is clear from what Marx wrote about materialistic determinism that he felt the control of the press would rest with those who owned the facilities — the presses, the paper, the broadcasting stations. So long as the capitalist class controls these physical properties, the working class will never have a fair access to the channels of communications. To have real access, the working class must own the means and facilities of mass communication, for the press, like other institutions of the state, is simply a class organ. And similarly, he must have felt that real freedom of the press could never exist except in the classless society, where the working class has seized the material properties of communication and has no more to fear from control by bourgeois owners. There is good reason to think that he did value such freedom, and wanted the conditions of "true freedom" to be created. Finally, one might suspect that freedom of the press must have been of less concern to Marx, as to his followers, than responsibility of the press. All these points will reappear in the following pages.

But since Marx has taken on the tone of gospel in many parts of the world, it is only proper to record here that on many key points his writings were incomplete or ambiguous, if not inconsistent. His ambiguities or inconsistencies arose mostly from the duality of his personality as scientist and evangelist. For even while he analyzed the historical process and diagnosed it as materialistically determined and inevitable, still he preached that through the right knowledge man could control destiny, and, as Muller says, "his own influence on modern history is the most spectacular example of the power of ideas and ideals" (105:312). In speaking of truth, he was a relativist, and many times argued the class bias of all thought; yet he insisted on the unexceptionable truth of his own theory of history. On many doctrinal points about which his followers speak with assurance and fire, Marx said practically nothing — for example, about the use of mass communication. But perhaps the most important of his omissions, in view of what happened later, was his failure to provide the revolution with a political theory, or even to say in any very specific terms what "dictatorship of the proletariat" should mean. That left it up to Lenin and Stalin to become architects of the Soviet state.

As this paper goes into proof, word comes of the address by Krushchev to the Supreme Soviet, denouncing Stalin. This is a most remarkable development, and the question at once arises, whether it portends any decisive change in the goals and architecture of the Soviet state. More particularly, it is necessary to ask whether this policy will negate any of the essential developments of the Soviet system which took place during Stalin's time, and which we shall describe in these next pages. We shall have to await developments, of course. But the indication now is that the fundamentals are left unchanged. The mood of Soviet foreign relations will change, but the purpose of Soviet foreign relations will not. The concept of "one leader" is probably dead for a while in the Soviet Union. The men in the Kremlin seem to be distributing the tasks and decisions of government among them, and it may well be that there will be some liberalizing of the amount of participation and criticism permitted the lower echelons of Party members. Additional contacts with the outside world will be encouraged, and it may be that surveillance will at least for a time be lessened. These are signs and tendencies only; it will take several years to see whether this new posture on the part of the Soviet leaders is a feint or a really new look. Meanwhile it must be assumed that the basic goals of the Soviet state and the basis of its control over communications, as developed under the long influence of Marx, Lenin, and Stalin, are not going to change. One of the best pieces of evidence for that assumption is a statement in *Pravda* for July 7, 1956: "The Communist Party has been and will be the only master of the minds and thoughts, the spokesman, leader and organizer of the people in their entire struggle for Communism." That would suggest that we are still dealing with the Marx-Lenin-Stalin pattern.

THE DEVELOPMENT THROUGH LENIN AND STALIN

Throughout all the years of preparation for revolution, the attention of Lenin and his followers had to be centered on the problems of seizing power. There was little time to think of the form Socialism would take *after* the revolution. George Kennan (in the essay he modestly signed "X") has analyzed this period of transition very well, and calls Lenin's ideas of the postrevolutionary future "for the most part nebulous, visionary, and impractical" (98:104). Beyond the nationalization of industry and the expropriation of large private capital holdings, he says, there was no agreed program. They were extremely vague on the treatment of the peasantry (who, in Marxist thought, are not part of the proletariat), and indeed their policy toward the peasants remained vague for many years after they came to power.

The Soviet state, therefore, developed slowly and uncertainly after October, 1917, and with many abrupt changes of line. We can say, from a few decades' vantage point, that the form and direction it took were products of ideology and circumstances and personalities. The *ideology*, of course, was inherited from Marx and Engels — the incomplete, ambiguous analysis of history in terms of material determinism and class struggle. The *circumstances* were such as to make dictatorial power a necessity. The Bolsheviks were never more than a tiny fraction of the people of Russia. The first abrupt attempt to eliminate private production and commerce was an abject failure. When controls were even slightly relaxed, it became evident that large sectors of society were waiting to step into the power and trade vacuum thus created. From the beginning of the Soviet state until today, as Kennan points out, this power has never been consolidated, and thus "the men in the Kremlin have continued to be predominantly absorbed with the struggle to secure and make absolute the power which they seized in November 1917" (98:106). The nature of *personalities* in the Kremlin has demanded that.

What kind of men were the leaders in the Kremlin? They were insecure and fanatical. They were Promethean; indeed, perhaps never before in history have so few men grasped such vast powers over so many, in such confidence that they knew exactly how to lead their subjects into the golden pastures. George Kennan has studied the Lenin-Stalin group as carefully as any man. Here is what he has to say about them:

Their particular brand of fanaticism, unmodified by any of the Anglo-Saxon traditions of compromise, was too fierce and too jealous to envisage any permanent sharing of power. From the Russian-Asiatic world out of which they had emerged they carried with them a scepticism as to the possibilities of permanent and peaceful coexistence of rival forces. Easily persuaded of their own doctrinaire "rightness," they insisted on the submission or destruction of all competing power. Outside of the Communist Party, Russian society was to have no rigidity. There were to be no forms of collective human activity or association which would not be dominated by the Party. . . . And within the Party the same principle was to apply. The mass of Party members might go through the motions of election, deliberation, decision and action; but in these motions they were to be animated not by their own individual wills but by the awesome breath of the Party leadership and the brooding presence of "the word."

Let it be stressed again that subjectively these men probably did not seek absolutism for its own sake. They doubtless believed — and found it easy to believe — that they alone knew what was good for society and that they could accomplish that good once their power was secure and unchallengeable. But in securing that security of their own rule they were prepared to recognize no restrictions, either of God or man, on the character of their methods.

And until such time as that security might be achieved, they placed far down on the scale of operational priorities the comforts and happiness of the peoples entrusted to their care (98:105-06).

Thus the combination of ideology, circumstance, and personalities combined to create on Russian soil one of the most complete dictatorships in modern history. This dictatorship emphasized such parts of the ideology as met its needs, and which instead of withering away as Marx had foreseen, has immensely expanded its bureaucracy and its instruments of surveillance and control. The elements of Marx it has come to emphasize have been the innate hostility between capitalism and socialism, and the infallibility of the leaders who have "the word" — that is, the Marxian word. It is obviously necessary for them to keep alive both the sense of danger and the sense of leadership. The part of the ideology which it has been most convenient to ignore is the famous picture of the withering away of the state once the proletariat has seized the material bases of power. Lenin himself never got around to correcting Marx on this point, and the job was finally left to Stalin who thus had the exceedingly embarrassing task of correcting *both* Marx and Lenin. He did so by saying that Lenin wrote his famous volume, *The State and Revolution,* with the intention of defending and clarifying Marx and Engels; and had intended to write a second volume of that work, summing up the principal lessons of the Russian experience. "There can be no doubt" (said Stalin) "that Lenin intended in the second volume of his book to elaborate and develop the theory of the state on the basis of his experience gained during the existence of Soviet power in our country. Death, however, prevented him from carrying this task into execution. But what Lenin did not manage to do should be done by his disciples" (113:658). Thus "under the protection of Lenin's ghost," as Hans Kelsen expresses it, Stalin stated the new doctrine of the Soviet state, which was essentially that in a strong state, military and police power would be needed as long as the Soviet Union is surrounded by capitalist powers. After the last remnants of the capitalist system had been eliminated in Russia, after a cultural revolution had been brought about, after a modern army had been formed for defense of the country, still the need for a strong government remained, said Stalin, because

In place of this function of suppression the state acquired the function of protecting Socialist property from thieves and pilferers of the people's property. The function of defending the country from foreign attack fully remained; consequently the Red Army and the Navy also fully remained, as did the punitive organs and the intelligence service, which are indispensable for the detection and punishment of the spies, assassins, and wreckers sent into this country by foreign espionage services. The function of economic organization and cultural education by the state organs also remained, and was developed to the full. Now the main task of our state inside the country is the work of peaceful economic organization and cultural education. As for our army, punitive organs and intelligence service, their edge is no longer turned to the inside of our country but to the outside, against the external enemies (113:661).

Side by side with the concept of a nonwithering Bolshevik state developed the concept of what might be called the Bolshevik ideal personality. In part this is a mirror image of the leaders, in part a synthesis of the same elements which went into the designing of the state. Margaret Mead has written incisively of it, and anyone who is interested may profitably read what she has to say in *Soviet Attitudes toward Authority* (104). This "Bolshevik ideal personality," she concludes, is a combination of eastern and western characteristics. To a certain extent, the Bolshevik ideal has characteristics in common with the Puritan fathers of New England and with many other religious groups at periods of ferment. That is, the Bolshevik ideal personality is highly goal-oriented, has a driving "conscience," and is able to produce an extremely high level of activity without external prodding. His performance is expected to be focused and meaningful, and his private feelings must be subordinated to the chief goals he serves. Even rest and relaxation are suspect, to a Bolshevik. So far, this is a not unfamiliar personality pattern. But the Bolshevik personality demands also a complete subjection of the individual to the control of the Party. Although the individual, says Dr. Mead, "is to have a strong internal conscience, yet the perception of the correct line of action is delegated to a small group of leaders, and the will of the individual is to be used first for the voluntary act of initial subjection and then to execute this truth perceived by the leadership" (104:29). Deviation from this path is regarded as peculiarly horrific, and a broad machinery of self-criticism and mutual criticism is set up to prevent and correct deviations. This is the kind of personality which the men around Lenin and Stalin have tried to build around *them*.

We have taken time to suggest these developing lines of Soviet ideology, government, and personality because it is manifestly impossible to understand the present situation in the Soviet Union solely on the basis of Marxism or solely on the basis of what Lenin and Stalin contributed to the Marxist tradition. Furthermore, it should be emphasized that Soviet mass communication was developing, during the period we have been talking about, as an *integral part* of the Soviet state. In the Soviet system, there is not a theory of the state and a theory of communication; there is only one theory. Nothing could be farther from Soviet thinking than our concept of the press as a Fourth Estate to watch and report on and criticize the first three. Mass communications, from the beginning of the proletarian revolution, were conceived of instrumentally. It was Lenin who said that the newspaper should be a "collective propagandist, collective agitator . . . collective organizer" (102:4, 114). The media were therefore instruments to be controlled by the state (on behalf of the people) through control of the material facilities of communication; private media thus went out of existence very early in Soviet history. The media should be used as instruments to convey the "word" as interpreted by the Kremlin. The media should be used as instruments of social change and social control, in a tightly unified, closely drawn frame of reference. Finally, the media should be instruments of serious purpose. Their use for recreation is considered an unworthy use, somewhat as, in the case of the Bolshevik man, relaxation is suspect. In other words, the Soviet media have grown so as to reflect the Soviet official ideology, the Soviet state, and the Soviet "ideal personality," as we shall see in the next pages.

2. FOREGROUND

THE THEORY NOW

Let us now try to describe the Soviet concept of mass communication as it has emerged from this long history. And let us remind ourselves that this concept of communication is integral with the concept of the Soviet state. Therefore, our first task must be to look at the more general theory.

The source of power

In Soviet theory, as I have elsewhere said (110), power is social, resident in people, latent in social institutions, and generated in social action. This power is at its maximum (a) when it is joined with natural resources and the facilities of production and distribution, and (b) when it is organized and directed.

Thus Lenin said, "The proletariat has no other weapon in the fight for power except organization . . . the proletariat can become and will become a dominant force only because its intellectual unity created by the principles of Marxism is fortified by the material unity of organization which welds millions of toilers into an army of the working class."

The source of leadership

The Communist Party possesses this power of organization. It therefore considers that it has the right to serve as advance guard and leader of the mass. As Vyshinsky says, "The political basis of the USSR comprises — as the most important principle of the worker-class dictatorship — the leading and directing role of the Communist Party in all fields of economic, social, and cultural activity. The works of Lenin and Stalin develop exhaustively the theoretical and organizational practical aspects of this matter" (116:159). But yet, as Selznick points out (112), the Party does not merely insert itself in a position of leadership of the masses; in a very real sense it creates the masses by organizing them — by establishing organs of access and control which transform a diffuse population into a mobilizable source of power.

The Party thinks of itself, therefore, as a kind of general staff for the mass of workers. It is custodian of basic doctrine, eyes and ears for the mass, guide into action (see 110). There is no doubt that the role of the Party has become more important, the role of the mass more passive, since the 1920's. When the mass accepts this guidance, it must also accept strict control. It has been observed that the Party operates on the Bonapartist assumption that delegation of authority to leadership places the leadership in unlimited control during its period of office. Therefore, attacks against leadership are equivalent to treason against the state. Purges are an accepted tool of governing. And the political apparatus must provide whatever control structure is necessary to mobilize and direct the energy of the mass.

How does the Party in practice exercise its leadership? Says Vyshinsky:

Practically, the party's guidance of the Soviets is actualized as follows: (1) First of all, the party seeks to advance its candidates into the basic posts of state work in our country at elections for Soviets — its best workers, devoted to the concerns of socialist building and enjoying the broadest confidence of the popular masses. In this the party succeeds. . . . (2) "The Party verifies the work of the organs of government and the organs of authority correcting unavoidable mistakes and shortcomings, helping them develop the decisions of the government and trying to guarantee them support of the masses — and not a single important decision is taken by them without corresponding directions of the Party." (3) "In developing a plan of work of a given organ of authority — whether along the line of industry and agriculture or that of building trade and culture — the Party gives general guiding directions defining the character and direction of the work. . . ." (116:160).

As the mass must submit to the dictatorship of the Party, so the Party must submit to the dictatorship of its central bureaucracy and leaders. Here as elsewhere appears the Bolshevik faith in organization, deriving from the need to organize in order to seize and maintain power. Lenin, for example, tells how he and his circle "suffered to the point of torture from the realization that we were proving ourselves to be amateurs at a moment in history when we might have been able to say. . . . 'Give us an organization of revolutionists and we shall overturn the whole of Russia!' " The kind of organization for which the Bolsheviks felt the need was a strictly monolithic party. No competing power structures, no substantial deviations in ideology, are permitted. Indeed, no other kind of structure could withstand the changes of tactics and the ceaseless combat required of the Party. As Stalin said, "the unexampled unity and compactness of our Party . . . made it possible to avoid a split on the occasion of a turn as sharp as the New Economic Policy. Not a single (other) party in the world . . . would have withstood such a sharp turn without confusion, without a split" (113:221).

The truth and the line. How is the "truth" derived for expression in the "line"? Throughout the years there has been a marked change in this respect. In the early years of Soviet power, as Margaret Mead notes (104:21), it was assumed that the truth was arrived at through collective deliberation of the Party. Therefore, each Party member was supposed to have full freedom of discussion until a Party Congress had reached a decision. As early as the 10th Congress, in 1921, however, Lenin expressed grave doubts about the efficiency of this system. During the 1920's control passed rapidly from the broad discussion and Party Congresses to the small group of top Party leaders. Before the end of the 20's — and ever since — Party Congresses are called chiefly to approve decisions already made. "The appropriate behavior of the Party member today," says Dr. Mead, "is to know the principles of Marxism-Leninism and to apply them as directed by the Line, not to think about them" (104:21).

One effect of this development is, therefore, to put basic responsibility for all mass communications in the hands of a small group of top Party leaders. All the mass media in the Soviet Union become speaking trumpets for these leaders, and the editors and directors listen anxiously for the latest Olympian rumblings of "the truth."

A second effect is to create a somewhat changeable line, with resulting insecurity in every Party member, for, as it has often been remarked, behavior which was true and loyal yesterday may be branded as false and disloyal tomorrow. As a student of Russia has observed, "a man whose particular scientific dogma has been in disgrace for a period of years may be suddenly brought back from an ignominious sojourn on the periphery — a mild form of exile — and made the head of an important institute or bureau. He may be publicly described as being entirely good, while the man he replaces, who may have received the same appointment with a comparable statement of his absolute loyalty and goodness five years before, is now unmasked as having been an 'enemy of the people,' or whatever the official terms of vilification may be. . . . The assumption that every human being is potentially and continuingly wholly good *and* wholly bad throughout life is grounded in traditional Russian character and complements political practice very neatly" (104:33).

Still a third result is to create what appears to the outside, at least, as a double standard of truth. On the one hand, the basic laws are considered absolute and unassailable. As Lenin said, "the teachings of Marx are immovable because they are true *(verno)*." And again, "truth *(istina)* is what corresponds to reality." Thus, basically the Soviets are committed to a material determinism, and to a concept of class struggle which must inevitably end with the victory of the proletariat. On issues like this, the idea of compromise, in our sense, is simply incomprehensible to the Soviet leadership. Thus, one American negotiator reported: "During negotiations they feel that appeals to public opinion are just a bluff. If American public opinion is contrary to what they want to do, our government or some hidden body, a capitalist Politburo, must be manipulating it. We think of compromise as a natural way to get on with the job, but to them compromise is usually coupled with the adjective rotten. They are puzzled by our emphasis on the desirability of compromise" (quoted, 104:15).

To the Soviet negotiator there are not "two sides to every question." There are only a focused and an unfocused lens on reality.

Thus, while on the one hand the basic concepts and goals are regarded as absolute and unchangeable, on the other hand communications tend to be judged not on the test of their objective truth but on the test of their impact. Do they contribute to the basic goals? Bolshevik doctrine, as Leites says, thus opposes the old tendency of the Russian intelligentsia to stress "sincerity" (100:123). Soviet spokesmen are expected to do what Tolstoy had reproached women for doing — use words, not to express their thoughts, but to attain their ends. Soviet diplomats are, in fact, expected to retreat at strategic moments (for example, to sign a treaty with Germany or to advocate world peace and coexistence) if those retreats are intended to contribute in the long run to basic goals. Soviet media are expected to change their line overnight, to denounce a man they previously lionized, or advocate a policy they had previously excoriated, if top leadership informs them that this is the *new* line. In the sense in which our newspaper editors talk about it, truth is irrelevant in the editing of a Soviet newspaper. On the other hand, compromise, majority opinion, a "middle of the road policy," all of which are so important to our communicators and political representatives, are questionable if not reprehensible to a Russian editor or politician.

The nature of the state. We are about to define Soviet mass communication as a spokesman for the line and an instrument of the state. Before taking up the mass media directly, therefore, we should properly say a few words about the Soviet state as it has evolved.

We have already said enough about the state to make clear its general nature — a dictatorship in which the power pyramid rises very sharply from the proletariat to a select Party to a select few leaders. There is no sign of the predicted "withering away" of the bureaucracy. As might be expected, it maintains tight controls over the resources, facilities, and relationships of production.

We should add that the Soviet state operates by simultaneous and coordinated programs of coercion and persuasion. The persuasion is the responsibility of agitators, propagandists, and the media. Lest it be thought that coercion would be inappropriate and persuasion unnecessary in the "Soviet socialist" society, the Soviet leaders point out that the present is a "transition" period. Thus Vyshinsky:

Suppression and the use of force by the state are still essential during the transition period — force, however, exerted by the exploited majority upon the exploiting minority, different in type and new in principle. . . .

The new Soviet state is a machine to crush the resistance of exploiters, to do away with exploitation and class domination by exploiters, to reinforce the class dominance of the proletariat and its leadership of the rest of the toiling masses to the end of finally liquidating classes in general and passing into communism. . . .

Hence follow the specific tasks of crushing the enemies of socialism and the particular significance of such methods of exposing and annihilating them as intensification of the revolutionary vigilance of the toiling masses and organs of proletarian dictatorship, intensified guard of the boundaries of the USSR, intensification of measures to thwart counterrevolutionary activity, and so on (116:3).

Mass communications in the Soviet state

We come now to the point where we can leave the background and the political framework and begin to talk directly about mass communication in the Soviet Union. And the first direct statements we have to make about Soviet communication will help to illustrate why it has seemed necessary to sketch in so much political and historical background. For in trying to define the present Soviet concept of mass communication, we have to say that

Mass communications are used instrumentally — that is, as an instrument of the state and the Party.

They are closely integrated with other instruments of state power and Party influence.

They are used as instruments of unity within the state and the Party.

They are used as instruments of state and Party "revelation."

They are used almost exclusively as instruments of propaganda and agitation.

They are characterized by a strictly enforced responsibility.

Let us talk about those points, one by one.

Instrumental use of mass communications. Marx undoubtedly dreamed of the press as free of the state, serving as a real spokesman of the people. And if the state had withered away, as predicted, after the revolution, perhaps his dream might have come true. There are vestiges of the dream even now, for example in the practice of Soviet leaders in operating their newspapers with very small professional staffs, apparently on the theory that "amateur" newspaper writers are to be encouraged. But actually the mass communication system in the present Soviet thinking is about as much an instrument as a typewriter or a megaphone. There is no place in the Soviet concept for the idea of the press as a clear and independent mirror of events. Nothing is farther from Soviet intention than giving mass communication units any of the responsibility for originating public opinion or pushing the state into a policy decision. A "personal paper," like the Chicago *Tribune* under Colonel McCormick, an independent critical journal like the New York *Times,* or opposing opinions on the same radio station such as one can hear in this country on ABC, are not within the Soviet concept. The communication system, like every other system in the Soviet state, exists to do a job specifically assigned it by the leaders of the state. Over-all, this job is to contribute to the advance of the working class and world Communism in the class struggle, and to maintain and advance the power of the Soviets. Specifically, the media are assigned certain tasks within that large assignment, which we shall now talk about in more detail. The point is, that Soviet mass communications do not have integrity of their own. Their integrity, such as it is, is that of the state. They are "kept" instruments, and they follow humbly and nimbly the gyrations of the Party line and the state directives.

Mass communications are integrated with other instruments. This makes it possible for the mass media to be integrated into the functioning of the state in a way which would be quite foreign to our own media. We tend to think of a number of parallel forces acting on American public opinion. These range from the interpersonal discussion within the primary group, through the organizations and the media reporting and discussing events, to the actions of the government. It is sometimes hard for us to grasp that in the Soviet state these forces are not parallel; they are *one.* That is, the group meetings at the block level, the youth meetings in school, the school system, the unions, the lower echelons of the Party, the papers, the broadcasts, the publishing industry, and the police and surveillance system of the government are different instruments with a single purpose. They are all saying the same thing.

Stalin defined political leadership as "the ability to convince the masses of the correctness of the Party's policy." But both Lenin and Stalin heaped scorn on Party members who depended on words alone. They insisted, in Lenin's words that "the dictatorship of the proletariat was successful because it knew how to combine compulsion with persuasion." Propaganda, agitation, organization, and coercion represent an unbroken continuum in their thinking. The media are designed specifically, not only to inform the people, but also to serve the agitators who are organizing the masses, the Party leaders in the communities, the industrial groups who use the papers for oral readings, the schools who use them on many occasions as textbooks. There is a great deal of sameness about the content of Soviet media on any day, and this is regarded as a strength, rather than a weakness. And the leaders of the state are in no doubt as to the limits of the effective use of the media. Lenin said: "As long as the question was (and insofar as it still is) one of winning over the vanguard of the proletariat to Communism, so long, and to that extent, propaganda took first place; even propaganda circles, with all the imperfections of the circles, are useful under these conditions and produce fruitful results. But when it is a question of the practical action of the masses, of the dispositions, if one may so express it, of vast armies, of the alignment of all the class forces of the given society for the final and decisive battle, then propaganda habits alone, the mere repetition of the truths of 'pure' Communism, are of no avail" (quoted, 112:9).

Mass communications as instruments for unity. From what we have just said it is apparent that one of the most prized abilities of the mass media in the Soviet state should be to contribute to the unity of the state. We have already mentioned how the Bolsheviks valued their "famed unity." The media are their swiftest instruments for achieving unity of knowledge within their own country. That is why the leaders have gone to such great troubles to establish controls and censorship over their own publications, broadcasts, and films, and to keep foreign publications, broadcasts, and films out of the country. That is also why the sameness of the Soviet media is regarded in the Soviets as a sign of health.

Mass communications as instruments of revelation. One special job, and one general job, are assigned the communicators of the Soviet state. We shall talk about the general task presently. The special job is to make "political revelations in every sphere." (The words are Lenin's.) What does he mean by these "revelations"? Domenach, who saw some of them at first hand, says they "consist of probing behind the façade of sophisms with which the ruling classes cloak their selfish interests, the true nature of their desires and the actual basis of their power, and of giving the masses a 'true picture' of them" (88:266). He then quotes Lenin on revelations: "The worker will not be able to get this true picture from books; he will not find it in any current accounts, in still-fresh explanations of things happening at any given moment, about which we speak or whisper among ourselves and which are reflected in such-and-such facts, figures, verdicts, etc. These political revelations, embracing all spheres, are the necessary and fundamental conditions of preparing the masses for their revolutionary activity" (102:1, 22).

In other words the job of the propagandist and the agitator (and the mass communicator) is to look at events from the Marxist-Leninist-Stalinist standpoint, go behind the appearance to the reality (reality being always defined in terms of the class struggle), and interpret the 'real meaning' of events to the masses. In so doing he grounds his explanations in real and believable tensions. He begins with details which are or seem verifiable. He proceeds from small irritations to interpretation on a grand scale. Domenach records how the French Communists "demonstrated" the "evils" of the "imperialist" Marshall Plan from the tiniest instances — a scarcity of some kind of goods, the closing of a factory, the reduction of water supply in a rural community. A strike, a political scandal, an instance of discrimination, an unwise statement by a public figure, a yearning for peace that will bring the young men home from military service — all these provide a chance for the communicator to work from the specific to the general doctrinal meaning, in the words of their own instructions to "tear the mask from the enemy."

This is the function which, in the Soviet concept of the mass media, largely replaces our own function of news gathering and news writing.

Mass communications as agitator, propagandist, organizer. The basic job of the mass media is, as we have suggested, to serve as collective agitator, propagandist, and organizer. Plekhanov is the author of the famous distinction, so often quoted, between agitation and propaganda. A propagandist, he said, presents many ideas to one or a few people; an agitator presents only one or a few ideas, but to a mass of people (108). Commenting on this distinction, Lenin said that the agitator will fasten his attention on a concrete injustice "engendered by the contradictions inherent in capitalism," and against that background "will endeavor to rouse mass discontent and indignation against the crying injustice, leaving to the propagandist the responsibility of giving a complete explanation for the contradiction. This is why the propagandist works principally through the written word and the agitator through the spoken word" (102:1, 226). In Communist thinking, therefore, there is no sharp dichotomy between agitator and propagandist. They are both needed in the combat party, and their words and their deeds fit into the organizing activities of the party.

Thus, the Soviet mass communication system is charged with working on three levels. It is to provide the popularized "revelations," by which to contribute to the political consciousness of the masses. It is to provide the doctrinal explanations by which to inform the leaders of thought. And by carrying a great deal of official information, it is to contribute to the smooth functioning of the Party and the organization of the workers.

Mass communications as responsible instruments: responsibility and freedom. There is no doubt that a high degree of responsibility is required of the operators of Soviet mass communications. Since this concept of responsibility is closely related to the Soviet concept of freedom, and since the Soviet use of these terms is somewhat different from ours, we are going to devote the whole following section to the relation of freedom and responsibility in Soviet media.

To us, the Soviet mass media look like closely controlled instrumentalities of the state. To the Soviet mind, our media are closely controlled instrumentalities of a capitalist class. In our view, the Soviet media are far from free; but the Soviet official position is that they are the freest in the world. What lies behind this fundamental conflict of opinion?

Let us begin with Article 125 of the Constitution of the USSR, which reads as follows:

In conformity with the interests of the working people, and in order to strengthen the socialist system, the citizens of the USSR are guaranteed by law:

(a) Freedom of speech;
(b) Freedom of the press;
(c) Freedom of assembly, including the holding of mass meetings;
(d) Freedom of street processions and demonstrations.

These civil rights are ensured by placing at the disposal of the working people and their organizations, printing presses, stocks of paper, public buildings, the streets, communications, facilities and other material requisites for the exercise of these rights.

Probably the best exposition of the meaning of this article from the Soviet point of view is by Andrei Vyshinsky, in *The Law of the Soviet State* (116:539ff.). Alex Inkeles also has some able comments on the meaning of the article, from our point of view, in *Public Opinion in Soviet Russia* (95:136ff.). These treatments are too long to quote, and in any case something may be gained by attempting a new approach which will draw on both these sources but handle the matter in a somewhat different way.

The key to the problem is obviously what the Soviets mean by the word *freedom* in this article, and whether there is a difference between their overt and covert viewpoints. From Marx to Bulganin we have a series of defenses of "freedom." For example, here is what Stalin said to Roy Howard in an interview:

Implicit in your question is the innuendo that socialist society negates individual freedom. That is not so. . . . We have not built this society in order to cramp individual freedom. We have built it in order that human personality might feel itself actually free. We built it for the sake of genuine personal freedom, freedom without quotation marks. What can be the "personal freedom" of an unemployed person who goes hungry and finds no use for his toil? Only where exploitation is annihilated, where there is no oppression of some by others, no unemployment, no beggary, and no trembling for fear that a man may on the morrow lose his work, his habitation, and his bread — only there is true freedom found (113).

Stalin in that passage, of course, is arguing the material basis of freedom. Bearing this in mind, let us try to put down a few statements about the Soviet concept:

1. From the Soviet point of view, absolute freedom is impossible.

As Lenin wrote, "to live in a society and be free from this society is impossible." "Truth is partisan," he said at another time. Therefore, the Soviet spokesmen consistently argue, as Inkeles recalls, that "in a society based on money, there can be no freedom from money" (95:136). They contend that papers in a capitalist society must necessarily express capitalist doctrine. They argue that any idea of objective news is nonsense and hypocrisy; by objective news we mean, they say, news that is slanted to maintain the capitalist status quo. Indeed, Russian communicators are sternly warned against "objectivity," which is thought to be turning from the one true line. Inkeles quotes Lenin as saying that the Soviet press would be free in that it would be free of "capital, careerism, and bourgeois anarchistic individualism." Nevertheless, it would make no claim to *independence,* but would be quite openly tied to the proletariat. In "one of those characteristically Bolshevik turns of phrase," says Inkeles, Lenin then stated that "the independence of the Bolshevik press rests in the closest dependence on the working class" (95:136). Thus we have good reason to suspect that the true and covert belief of the Communists is simply that *no* press is free. Their arguments about the freedom of

their own press would appear to be strictly for official consumption.
2. From the Soviet point of view, what is worth while is freedom to
say what *they* conceive to be truth.

That is, they say that the freedom we boast of is a purely negative
one: it is a freedom from interference by the state. The Soviet
people, on the other hand — their apologists say — have freedom
to express themselves *within* the bounds and limits of the state. As Muller noted, the Soviets say that for them "the state is not a necessary
evil against which the individual must be protected: it is a positive
good, a great co-operative enterprise that alone makes possible a fuller
life for the individual" (105:317). According to this viewpoint, then,
the difference is that the Anglo-American world is seeking freedom
from the state; whereas the Soviet citizen is enjoying his freedom
within the allegedly beneficent state which protects him in doing
"what is good for him." As has been several times remarked, anyone
can seem free even in an authoritarian system if he accepts the postulates and practices of the state. But from our point of view, no one
can really be free unless he is free to question the basic postulates of
the society in which he lives.

3. Therefore, in the Soviet Union no freedom *against the state* can
be permitted.

Says Vyshinsky: "In our state, naturally, there is and can be no
place for freedom of speech, press, and so on for the foes of socialism.
Every sort of attempt on their part to utilize to the detriment of the
state — that is to say, to the detriment of all toilers — these freedoms
granted to the toilers must be classified as a counterrevolutionary
crime. . . . Freedom of speech, of the press, of assembly, of meetings,
of street parades, and of demonstrations are the property of all the
citizens of the USSR, fully guaranteed by the state upon the single
condition that they be utilized in accord with the interests of the
toilers and to the end of strengthening the socialist social order"
(116:617).

The Soviet spokesmen are quite candid about this matter. They feel
it is their duty to protect Soviet citizens from all influences which
would interfere with their living within and being content with the
true doctrine and the beneficent state, as set forth by Party leaders.
The Iron Curtain follows quite naturally from this point of view. So
also does the liquidation or disfranchisement of the remnants of
the bourgeois class. They feel they must protect their citizens, as
Muller says, "from powerful, irresponsible men who want to promote

their own selfish interests at the expense of others, and who in the democracies largely own the 'free' press. Its gifted citizens, one might add, will also be free from the romantic fallacies of the west, such as André Gide's dictum that the great artist is necessarily a nonconformist. Its artists and intellectuals will work better because, like the Greeks, they are working with and for the community" (105:308).

"So runs the theory, on paper," he adds. What seems to them a "positive" freedom seems to us a negative conformity which is enforced, and which permits only the tiniest deviations from political, social, and cultural viewpoints closely controlled by a few men in the Kremlin. How far this caretaker and guide concept is below Marx's vision for man!

4. By owning the facilities, the Soviet guarantees access, and eliminates concealed class controls.

The Soviet spokesmen call our press not a free press, but rather a class-dominated one. Vyshinsky scoffs at the "bourgeois public law" concept that absence of preliminary censorship guarantees freedom of the press (116:612-13). He points out that in the United States and England, where precensorship has long been abolished, "the bond between press and capital, the enslavement of the press by capital, appears perhaps more closely than in any others." He mentions a number of examples — the London *Times* which he says is "the organ of banks, connected through its directors with Lloyd's bank, with the largest railroad companies, with insurance companies. . . ." He pays his respects also to the Hearst papers, the head of which, he says, is "a big American capitalist, connected with industry, banks, and concerns which are exploiting the countries of Latin and South America. . . . [and which] Carry on a bloodthirsty agitation against the Communist Party, the revolutionary workers' movement and the USSR." Freedom of the press, Vyshinsky concludes, "consists essentially in the possibility of freely publishing the genuine, not the falsified opinions *of the toiling masses,* rather than in the absence of preliminary censorship" (116:613).

It is clear that this emphasis on majority-class control of the facilities of publishing is merely official viewpoint, since the Bolsheviks always knew that the majority was not on their side, but claimed that history made them the proper agents of the majority. For overt argumentative purposes, the Soviet contends that freedom of communication goes with ownership of the physical properties of communication. It is contended that this ownership is held by only a few in the

United States, by most in the Soviet Union, hence (by this reasoning, at least) the Soviet press is a great deal freer. On the other hand, we point out that our press has the right to talk about the government in a way that no Russian paper can. "But your press is not free to talk freely about the working class and the world revolution," the Russians answer. It is the old argument of Marx vs. Mill, and there is little meeting place between the extremes.

5. Freedom and responsibility are inseparably linked in Soviet theory.

Recall that Article 125 of the Soviet constitution, which we have just quoted, began by saying freedoms were granted "in conformity with the interests of the working people and in order to strengthen the socialist system." The *results* of communication are always in the Soviet eye. As Inkeles says, we in this country tend to value the right of freedom of expression, the *right itself* in the abstract; and we usually permit no consideration except the most serious matters of national security or other human rights to limit us in the exercise of that right. That is why the Soviet spokesmen call ours an irresponsible press. We call theirs a controlled press because someone other than the communicator determines what is "in conformity with the interests of the working people" and "what strengthens the socialist system." First of all, the Soviet press is thus expected — indeed, compelled — to be responsible. First of all, the Anglo-American press is expected — indeed, enjoined — to speak freely. As Inkeles says in summing up this distinction,

it is declared to be the responsibility of the press in the Soviet Union to see that elections are a success for the party, that the labor productivity of the people is high, and so on. If in serving these ends the press also provides an opportunity for people to enjoy freedom of the press, well and good; but this consideration of freedom is secondary in the Soviet Union to the responsibilities of the press, and may be sacrificed if need be. In the United States the emphasis is placed on freedom rather than on responsibility. Freedom of expression is the absolute value, at least for those who have the means to express themselves; if in so doing they advance the common weal or otherwise act to advance certain social goals and fulfill responsibilities to the society, that too is well and good. But this consideration of the common good is secondary to the freedom of expression and may, if need be, be sacrificed to that freedom (95:138).

Here, as at so many other points, we have a theoretical difference which is all but insurmountable. But the difference can be understood. And perhaps the essential point to remember is that the mass communications which seem to us to be highly authoritarian and closely controlled, can be made in Soviet terminology to look like a free and responsible system because the majority class has the right and privilege of using them to express the "true Line" and to accomplish results which are allegedly for the good of his class and his state.

THE SYSTEM GROWS OUT OF THE THEORY: 1. THE PRINTED MEDIA

Before the October revolution of 1917, there were less than 1,000 newspapers in Russia. There are now more than 7,000, in addition to hundreds of thousands of typewritten and handwritten newspapers posted on walls or handed out in groups. There has likewise been a great increase in the number of magazines. The Soviet book industry, which was very modest indeed in the days of the Tsars, has now become one of the largest in the world, and this year will produce more than one billion books in more than 100 of the languages of the Soviet Union. It is clear that the Soviet press has taken seriously Lenin's injunction that it should be collective agitator, propagandist, and organizer for the masses.

In many respects, Soviet newspapers look strange and unfamiliar to a person who is used to the American press. For one thing they are a specialized press. Our newspapers are, for the most part, a generalized press.[1] There are in the United States a few labor papers, a few religious papers, but most of our newspapers are distinguished only by virtue of being large or small, daily or weekly. In the Soviet Union, almost half the newspapers are agriculture papers. Nearly 200 papers exist wholly for young people and children. There is a large Party press, a military press, a trade union press, a factory press.

One thing to remember is that this Soviet press is a planned press. Ours has "just grown." More precisely, it has grown according to the laws of public demand and private enterprise supply. But the Soviet press has been carefully distributed over the Union so as to serve the largest number of readers in the largest number of specialized ways. That is to say that the press is specialized both horizontally and vertically. Vertically, as we have pointed out, there are different kinds of papers to serve different kinds of affiliations and occupations. Horizontally, newspapers form into a huge pyramid, at the top of which are such all-union papers as *Pravda* (the organ of the Central

---

[1] Our magazine press, on the other hand, is more extensive and specialized than the Soviet one.

Party Committee) and *Izvestiya* (the organ of the Supreme Soviets), which circulate throughout the Soviet Union. At the next level are provincial papers which circulate throughout the territories and regions. Still lower on the pyramid are the local papers, serving districts and cities, state farms and factories. And at the very bottom are the wall and bulletin board newspapers. The number of newspapers increases, as we go down the pyramid. That is, there are only about 25 all-Union newspapers, about 500 provincial papers, and about 7,000 local papers. Circulations, however, decrease as we move down the pyramid, from *Pravda* (between two and three million) to the shop newspaper which may be typed out in only one copy for the bulletin board.

Resist the temptation to shrug your shoulders at a newspaper which has a circulation of one. The Soviets do not shrug their shoulders at it. They count and review these wall newspapers, and consider them an important part of their planned structure. And indeed they are, because they represent the farthest step the press can take in relating the central Line to the problems of a locality or a group. These wall newspapers are assigned a job which is too specific for *Pravda;* they are to translate *Pravda* and Marx-Lenin-Stalin into the words and worries of a few hundred Soviet citizens. The editor of *Pravda* may know Marx better. The editor of the wall newspaper will know his audience better.

The Soviet press is not only meticulously organized and spread over the Soviet Union; it is also meticulously supervised and controlled. This we must look at in some detail.

Control of Soviet print

Chief responsibility for control of the Soviet press belongs to the Party. Significantly it does not belong to the government. The government has a division of censorship, called *Glavlit,* an abbreviation of the Russian title of Chief Administration for Literary Affairs and Publishing. *Glavlit,* however, does not censor the publications of the Party at any level, nor the books of the Unified State Publishing House (*Ogiz*), nor the organ of the Supreme Soviets (*Izvestiya*). This obviously eliminates most of the Soviet press from the ministrations of *Glavlit.*

As a matter of fact, the government does not even have a department of public information. This function is carried on by the Department of Propaganda and Agitation of the Party. There is a central

Department under the immediate supervision of the Central Committee in Moscow, and subsidiary Departments at each level of the Party.

The reason why this responsibility is given to the Party rather than the government is completely in accord with theory. The government is supposed to wither away. The press is supposed to belong to the people, whose representative the Party is. Furthermore, the Soviet leaders have always placed very high importance on the Party as a custodian of values and determiner of goals, and on the press as "a transmission belt between the masses and the Party." Stalin said, "The press is the prime instrument through which the Party speaks daily, hourly with the working class in its own indispensable language. No other means such as this for weaving spiritual ties between Party and class, no other tool so flexible, is to be found in nature."

The Party exercises its control in three ways. In the first place its Departments of Propaganda and Agitation at various levels appoint editors and the Central Committee's Department of Propaganda and Agitation confirms the appointments. Their first consideration is, of course, to get a politically reliable appointee. At the beginning of the Soviet Union, when editorial skills were scarce, it was usually necessary to put Party members into editorial jobs almost wholly on the basis of their political reliability and knowledge of Marxism. Although the professional level of the Soviet press has greatly improved, still there is no doubt that political rather than professional reliability is the basic qualification for a Soviet editor. Inkeles quotes the names of the courses offered Soviet newspapermen, and the chapter titles of their textbooks, in order to demonstrate that what we think of as "editorial skill" is a very small part of the training of a Soviet editor. Rather, his training is in Marxist theory, Party history, and world politics.

In the second place, the Party issues, through its Department of Propaganda and Agitation, a very large number of directives as to what material is to appear in the press and how it is to be handled. A considerable part of the content of the press is what we would call handouts — letters to and from leading figures in the Party hierarchy and the government, public addresses, and official documents. Directions for handling other subjects are often in great detail.

In the third place, the Party reviews and criticizes the press. This responsibility is taken very seriously. At each level of the Party, there is a committee which samples and criticizes the press of its corresponding level. *Pravda* maintains a running criticism of the press. The top Party papers of various specialized kinds often criticize the lower levels of specialized press; for example, the top trade union or military papers criticize the lesser ones. Add to this formal criticism the constant *samokritika* — self criticism by the Soviet people — which is an old and honored Soviet custom, and which keeps a flow of letters finding fault with the performance of the press in a given instance, and you have a situation in which the Soviet press is under constant and thorough scrutiny.

It has often been pointed out that the position of a Soviet editor is by no means entirely enviable. His responsibility is to apply the Line to problems and audiences as he knows them. The larger his problem — for example, in the regions, or the various Soviet Socialist Republics — the more likely he is to deviate, or to run into a situation in which the Line is not altogether clear. Furthermore, he has to be nimble to keep up with some of the gyrations of the official Line. One serious mistake, and his career is over.

There is little doubt that many Soviet editors operate under considerable tension. But beyond that, what do they think of the job of editing a "people's paper"? What is it like to edit a paper where one is concerned not with facts but with dialectic, not with timely events but with the "Line"? One of the best descriptions of that experience comes from Arthur Koestler. "Gradually I learned to distrust my mechanistic preoccupation with facts and to regard the world around me in the light of dialectic interpretation," he said. "It was a satisfactory and indeed blissful state; once you had assimilated the technique you were no longer disturbed by facts; they automatically took on the proper color and fell into their proper place. Both morally and logically the Party was infallible: Morally, because its aims were right, that is, in accord with the Dialectic of History, and these aims justified all means; logically, because the Party was the vanguard of the Proletariat, and the Proletariat the embodiment of the active principle in History."

Content of the Soviet press

The Soviet newspaper press looks strange to us, for one thing, because it carries almost no advertising, as might be expected in a country where private enterprise does not exist. It looks even stranger because of its editorial content. In our sense, it can hardly be called a *news*paper at all. News to us means recent events. News to the Soviet editors means interpretation of social processes. As Inkeles points out in his lucid discussion, our focus is on the event; the flow of events is what our papers mirror; and the triviality of the event can sometimes be compensated for by its timeliness or by what we call "human interest." On the other hand, quoting Inkeles again, "the major, and in a sense virtually the only, news item in the Soviet Union is the process called socialist construction, that is, the general effort to build up Soviet society."

Events are regarded as news only in so far as they can meaningfully be related to that process. Thus, the Soviet press in the mid-thirties could for months devote the major part of its total space to discussions of the Stakhanovite movement, because of the importance which rationalizing production was held to have for increasing labor productivity. Or, to take an example from the field of ideology, it is literally beyond conception that a newspaper like the New York *Times* would devote almost half of its column space for a week to a national conference of biologists which had met to formulate a basic "ideological" policy for the "scientific" work of American biologists and to affirm the essentially American character of the environmental as against the hereditary approach to genetics. Yet this is precisely what *Pravda* did during one week of August, 1948, in relation to a conference of Soviet biologists (93 139-40).

The brutal truth is that providing timely news is a very small part of the work of a "collective propagandist, agitator, organizer," which is what the editor is trying to be. To the Soviet mind there must be a great sameness about events. The editor can pick and choose amongst his reports as he needs them to illustrate the social process he is trying to teach his readers. He need not present a given event soon after it occurs, because other events may just as well illustrate what he is trying to teach. A great deal of his paper is not news at all: it is "service" material for the Party, for factory and farm workers who are expected to increase productivity, for "reading hours" in local communities or schools. In a very real sense, the Soviet editor must feel that he is in control of events, whereas the American editor feels at the mercy of events. The American editor will tear up his pages in order to insert an important story as late as a few minutes before press time; the Soviet editor, on the other hand, can often plan his "content and layout one month in advance," and . . . have 50 per cent of each current issue set in type and made up several days before the issue date" (95:140-141).

American observers are often astonished at the smallness of Soviet newspaper staffs. As we have already suggested, this has two reasons.

One is the large amount of material furnished and the frequent direction given by Central Committee sources. Another is the importance placed by the Departments of Propaganda and Agitation on using a large amount of material written by "amateurs." And it is true that a typical Soviet paper may derive as much as a quarter to one half of its copy from individuals who have no connection with the staff whatsoever, but who contribute samokritika, interpretive articles, or discussion of Marxian theory.

According to the Soviet official viewpoint, therefore, their press is a magnificent experiment in creating "the people's press," owned and controlled by the representatives of the people, and used to make a better society for the people on the "One True Model." From our viewpoint (and possibly, the covert viewpoint of the Soviet leaders) it is a tightly controlled press used, not to serve the people but to do things to them, not to let them choose and decide, but to decide for them and then convince them without giving them an opportunity to choose otherwise.

THE SYSTEM: 2. BROADCASTING

Of all the media, only radio and television are younger than the Soviet Union. Broadcasting, therefore, is the only part of mass communication which the Soviet government has had an opportunity to develop entirely according to its own blueprint. The nature of this development is consequently of considerable interest to us.

Broadcasting in the Soviet Union is a large system as European and Asiatic systems go. There are somewhere in the neighborhood of 15 million receivers, counting crystal sets, and a sufficient number of national and regional stations to serve all these. Television is still at an early stage of growth. This growth has been rapid in the last year, however, and there are now about one million sets and about 25 transmitting stations.

But the interesting thing to us is the kind of use the Soviets make of their broadcasting. To get the full flavor of it, let us recall the various reactions when radio or television is about to come into an American community. The citizens of the community are looking forward to high quality entertainment in their own homes, to a quick source of news, to "reserved seats" (in their own living rooms) at special public events, plays, and operas, and — at least a few of them — to the kind of information we deal with in "educational broadcasting." The advertisers are looking forward to a new market. The government is not particularly concerned at all, except in the distribution of channels and in making sure that none of the neighboring channels are being violated. But let us now suppose that radio or television is coming into a Soviet community. The advertiser is not interested, because there is almost no advertising. The citizen is interested, but not chiefly for the reason that the medium will provide entertainment, because entertainment is not the chief purpose of Soviet broadcasting. The Soviet radio will bring in a quantity of good music, and television will carry concerts, ballets, and plays, but for the most part Soviet broadcasting will *talk* to its audiences. It will be the voice of the Party and of the government in the home. And, therefore, it is the Communist Party and the Soviet government which are chiefly concerned with the expansion of broadcasting in the Soviet Union, for they recognize the power and convenience of being able to communicate directly and instantly with so many of their people.

When we read the radio "decisions" — by which we mean the directives issued to the broadcasters in the Soviet Union — we find a great similarity to the tone of press "decisions." Radio, like press, is conceived of as having an instrumental, rather than a service function. For example, here is what the Party tells the broadcaster who is just taking up his new responsibility: "Possessing an audience of millions and penetrating to the most far-flung and 'deaf' corners of our immense country, the Soviet radio must carry to the widest masses the teachings of Marx-Lenin-Stalin, must raise the cultural-political level of the workers, must daily inform the workers of the success of socialist construction, must spread the word about the class struggle taking place throughout the world" (95:264). Broadcasting is expected also to contribute to the general education and improvement of the Soviet citizen, especially "in the realms of hygiene and sanitation, basic science, and techniques of production." And finally, it is expected to "provide the population with a positive and constructive means of relaxation" (93:263).

What is a "positive and constructive" means of relaxation? That is the yardstick which has determined whether many a Soviet broadcaster and publisher should be publicly criticized and deposed. Inkeles quotes Tamarkin, in his review of Soviet radio, as saying: "We renounce the broadcast of material whose only purpose is to divert the radio listener without consideration of the significance of the content of the given fact. Such things we regard as unhealthy trickery." He goes on to cite the Rostov station which "seemed unable to find time to broadcast certain 'glorious revolutionary news' from Spain, but seemed to have no trouble in finding a spot for some 'twaddle' about a man living somewhere in Africa who had reached the age of 146 years" (95: 266). In other words, what we think of as "human interest" is not positive and constructive in the Soviet sense. Neither are radio nor television comedians, unless they are satirizing the capitalist system. Neither are soap operas, unless they are on the theme of "socialist construction." In other words, here is deadly serious broadcasting, missionary broadcasting. It carries good music. But chiefly it is a teacher and a lecturer. It tells millions what the agitators would tell them face to face, if it were possible to reach them. When it talks about individuals, they tend to be heroes of the Soviet state, or villains of the opposition. When it talks about business or economics, it explains the Marxist view. When it talks about events which have local or colorful interest, it tries always to relate them to the basic processes of society as Marxists understand those processes.

In this respect, broadcast practice is exactly like press practice. The broadcaster, like the editor, is taught that events unless related to broad Marxist interpretation of history, are "trivia." Timeliness, even with broadcasting, is secondary. The focus is always on the broad stream of history interpreted in terms of the class struggle.

The system and its controls

The nature of the system need not detain us long. A group of Moscow stations, beamed to various parts of the Soviet Union, broadcast nearly around the clock, and act as network headquarters. Inkeles points out that their function is about like that of London to the BBC, or the New York station to United States networks. Most of the republics and regions have their own stations, which relay some of the Moscow transmissions and add some programs of their own. In particular, these regional stations are responsible for serving the many language groups within their receiving areas. Any of these stations may be received either directly on an individual receiver, or by the master receiver of a radio-diffusion network. These radio-diffusion networks represent really a third level of broadcasting. They consist of a master receiver, an amplifier, and wires which lead to loud speakers in homes, places of work, and public squares. The persons in charge of the master receiver may originate a certain number of their own programs and thus, like the local and wall newspapers, come as close as possible to meeting the specific needs of local listeners. But principally the radio-diffusion network is an ingenious device for putting radio (and perhaps television also) into the maximum number of places at the lowest cost and under the most secure control. There are millions of wired speakers in the Soviet Union.

It is obvious that the diffusion networks are easier to control than other listening because the listener has no choice of program. He cannot tune his receiver. In this and other ways, the Party goes to even greater lengths to insure its control of broadcasting than to insure its control of the press. Broadcasting is under the supervision of an All-Union Radio Committee, which is in turn controlled by the Party. At the republic and regional levels, and again at the level of the diffusion network, there are similar Radio Committees, in charge of broadcasting on their levels. The Party controls all broadcasting, by the same three means we have already described in terms of the press — that is, by inserting its own reliable members in all key appointments, by issuing a large number of directives and instructions, and by constant review and criticism. Threats and persuasion are used to keep the Soviet listener from tuning in foreign broadcasts. And in case any Soviet listeners should still be tempted, a vast network of jamming stations — estimated at more than 1,000 in the Soviet Union and her satellites — is at work day and night trying to blot out the foreign signals coming over the Iron Curtain.

THE SYSTEM: 3. FILM

It would be easy, in discussing the Soviet film, simply to write "ditto" under what has already been said about Soviet press and broadcasting. But the situation is not quite the same, for the Bolsheviks recognized from the beginning the essentially *art* nature of the film. Lenin spoke of its "spiritual influences," which seems an unlikely phrase to come from that source. And there has been a long history of experimentation in which Soviet propagandists and producers have tried to harness the aesthetic element in the film to the Marxist responsibility enjoined on all Soviet communications.

All the Soviet leaders have emphasized the teaching quality of the film. Inkeles quotes Lenin as saying that the film must deal with science and production as well as with comedy and drama, "and all this must be directed toward a single unitary goal — the struggle for the new life, for new customs, for a better future, for the blossoming of science and art." He called the film a "pictorial publicist," "a pictorial public lecture," and "artistic propaganda for our ideas in the form of an absorbing picture" (95:307). Stalin said the film is "a great and invaluable force . . . aiding the working class and its Party to educate the toilers in the spirit of socialism, to organize the masses . . . and to raise their cultural and political battle-fitness" (95:307). In other words, the basic assignment to the film was the same as that of press and broadcast — to serve as propagandist, agitator, organizer.

But the aesthetic element has continued to present a special problem. Comedy, for one thing, has always been hard to handle. The Minister of Cinematography admitted that "it is unquestionably very difficult to produce comedies which are simultaneously both gay and sapient" (95:311). In practice, it has often been found safer not to attempt comedies or other light films. And indeed the subject matter of Soviet films has shifted in a way that would make a very interesting study by itself. These shifts have apparently come from related forces — the trends and currents in art literature, the trends in audience tastes (it is notable that Soviet audiences have been reported as staying away from documentary films), and, most important, the shifting ideas of the Central Committee on the particular needs at the moment. Inkeles has a good review of this changing pattern of subject matter (95:308-09).

The Party controls films by the same means as press and broadcast. The central responsibility is given to the Agitprop Department of the Central Committee, and to the subsidiary groups at each Party level. These criticize, review, instruct the film makers, and also control the influx of foreign films and the choice of films to be shown. Cooperative associations of producers at the national and regional levels are well infiltrated by Party members, and in any case subject to the control and direction we have mentioned.

RELATION TO OTHER AUTHORITARIAN SYSTEMS

From our point of view, at least, the Soviet system is an authoritarian one — indeed, one of the most closely controlled systems in history. The question, therefore, arises: how is it different from the authoritarian systems discussed earlier in this volume, and from such modern authoritarianism as was represented by Nazi Germany?

The most obvious thing to say, in comparing Soviet authoritarianism with the authoritarianism of England before the Enlightenment, or with the modern survivals of that authoritarianism in many Free World countries today — the obvious thing to point out is that in the Soviet system the media are state-owned, whereas in the other authoritarian systems they are for the most part privately owned. Broadcasting systems are often state-owned, and occasionally one of the authoritarian countries will control the book industry or publish papers or magazines of its own. But typically the media in these countries are privately owned, though carefully controlled by patents, licensing, guilds, government pressure, and censorship. The result may be approximately the same, so far as the political content of the media goes; the Soviet system, as we have seen, is controlled by ownership, Party personnel in key positions, directives, review, criticism, and censorship. But in the authoritarian systems outside the Soviet countries, the media are typically part of the business system, and, to that extent, less exclusively an instrument of the government. The older authoritarian media were in bondage to the state, whereas the Soviet media are *in* and *of* the state.

But that is not enough to explain the very real differences between these systems and concepts. Let us recall some other, and perhaps more significant differences:

1. The Soviet system has removed the profit motive from publishing and broadcasting. Thus the media are free to do their duties as instruments of the state and Party, rather than as competitors for public favor. The rewards of ownership are not in advertising and circulation returns, but in effects on the public mind. The rewards of management are not in the by-products of prosperity, but in the by-products of orthodoxy and skill in propaganda. The decision as to success or failure tends to rest, not with the public, but with a few custodians of the Line and the Power.

2. The Soviet system has defined the function of mass communications positively; the older authoritarianism limited it negatively. That is, in typical authoritarian countries, the press is not permitted to do a number of things, largely related to criticism of the regime. In the Soviet system, the emphasis is rather on *requiring* the press to do certain things. The Soviets have moved beyond forbidding the press to criticize the regime, to the point actually that they are fairly free in inviting criticism of the minor functioning and functionaries of the regime. But the emphasis is on what the press is required to do — for

example, to increase the "political awareness" of the masses, to rally the population in support of the leaders and their program, to raise the level of efficiency of the workers, etc. In other words, the Soviet communications are wholly instrumental; in the older authoritarianism, the media were permitted, within limits, to determine their own level of service and function.

3. More than the older authoritarian systems, the Soviet system was built as a part of change, and to help accomplish change. The tasks of "exposing" the bourgeois, aiding in "socialist construction," "elevating" the workers, revealing the "evil machinations" of capitalism and furthering the final overthrow of capitalism and the coming of the classless society, have always been assigned the mass media. The older authoritarian systems, on the other hand, were primarily controlled with the idea of maintaining the status quo. The regime in power was anxious to avoid criticism and exposures which might affect its position. It is true that the Soviet system was to maintain the *Soviet* status quo, but always in a context of change and development.

4. There is a more general way for stating some of these differences. That is to say simply that the Soviet reasons for an authoritarian policy toward the mass media were considerably different than those of the older authoritarian states. The Soviet actions were based on economic determinism, rather than divine right. The Soviet authoritarianism was built on a concept of class warfare, and aimed at the dominance of one class, and ultimately at a classless society. The older authoritarianism, as we have previously said, was based on a strict class system which was intended to persist, with lower classes paying desired service to the ruling class. And the Soviet system has in it the seeds of change. The system is so designed that if the state were really to wither away, mass communication could continue under the guidance of the Party or whatever organization represented the single class. There was no such provision for change in the older systems.

5. Finally, it is obvious that Soviet mass communications are integrated into the total communication system and into the total government, in a way that authoritarian systems never were. The Soviet system is a *planned* system; the older ones, controlled systems. Soviet mass communications blend smoothly into Party and auxiliary organizations, word of mouth agitation, control and surveillance machinery. The chief newspaper of the Ukrainian Soviet Socialist Republic is thus like a soldier in the ranks of the Soviet state, who takes orders through established channels, marches with the other soldiers, and

derives significant color and personality from the whole army. In the older system, on the other hand, few of the mass media were integrated. The chief London paper in the seventeenth century would have had its own private personality, limited only by what it could discuss. In a sense it was an instrument of the regime, but was integrated into the activities of the regime as in no such sense is the Ukrainian paper. That kind of integration was a device that came to be accepted and perfected only in our own century, and the Bolsheviks and Nazis showed the way.

That leads us to talk briefly about Nazi mass communications. It is too easy and not very helpful to iump the Nazi and Soviet systems together under the term "totalitarian." If one thinks of the three chief systems discussed in this book — the old authoritarianism, the libertarian, and the Soviet — as three points of a triangle, then the Nazi system belongs somewhere on the side of the triangle between old authoritarian and Soviet. In some respects it is more like one, in other respects more like the other. Let us compare some aspects of the Nazi authoritarianism with the Soviet.

1. Obviously, the two systems operated under widely different philosophical assumptions. The Soviet system was built on Marx and Engels, with Hegel's dialectic "inverted," and some admixture of older Russian thinking. The Nazis built on Hegel (*not* inverted), on Kant's philosophy of duty, and Fichte's nationalism. In place of the materialistic determinism of the Soviets, the Nazis had a kind of mysticism about their thinking, a somewhat foggy reliance on spirit, racial inheritance, and the "right idea" which compares and contrasts interestingly with the Soviet confidence in having the "right Line" direct from Marx. It is noteworthy, however, how often these systems started from completely different sources and came out with identical tactics. Thus, for example, the Nazis were as scornful of "objectivity" as are the Soviets. Hadamovsky, Goebbels' deputy, said: " 'Impartiality' is a threat to any weak character. The 'objective press' is 'all in favor of anything national'; but . . . not for those who want to realize nationalism by uniting under some name or other. . . . The kind of press which bred this kind of men (it calls itself free, independent, neutral, non-partisan, supra-partisan, and objective) must either change or disappear from the German scene. There is only one object worthy of the great effort of the press, namely, the nation" (92). And of the *Volkische Beobachter,* the official Nazi paper, he said: "Contrary

to the ambitions of the liberal newspapers who think that the world revolves around them, the National-Socialist propaganda organ is neither trying to be a news sheet, nor does it care to be objective, free, and independent" (92). The vocabulary is different, but the sentiment is familiar.

2. For the most part, the Nazis permitted their mass media to remain under private ownership. In this respect, they were more like the older than the Soviet authoritarianism.

3. On the other hand, the Nazi system was more like the Soviet in that it was an instrumentalized and more closely integrated system. Like the Soviet system, too, it was used to bring about change — to bring the Nazis into power, to re-educate and re-mold the German people, to aid the Nazi armies. The Nazi system was inevitably different from the Soviet because of the difference in the way it came into being, and the circumstances of its use. Thus, the Bolsheviks came into power by means of quick and violent revolution. They had to fight for power, but were in a position to establish a system of control and a planned communication network. The Nazis, on the other hand, came into power gradually and for the most part through orderly means. They inherited a communication system much more fully developed than the Soviet system. The fact that for a long time they had little access to the mass media led them to perfect the technique of the mass meeting. Like the Bolsheviks they early saw the importance of a party organization, and developed a militant combat party. But for the most part they were in a position of trying to take a system already developed, and *use* it as an instrument of state. The Bolsheviks were able to build such a system, and more fully integrate it.

4. The Nazis, like the Bolsheviks, came to depend on a combination of coercion and persuasion. The Nazi phrase was "ideas, propaganda, and power." Many of their control devices were precisely parallel to those of the Bolsheviks — for example, inserting Party members into key communication jobs, issuing policy directives, threats, surveillance. They made sure of dominance of the "arteries" of communication — for example, the wire news service and the radio networks. The press bothered them in a way it never bothered the Soviets, probably because the Nazis never took over the press, and the German tradition of a free and outspoken press was too strong to be silenced by threats and minor coercion alone. Hadamovsky and Goebbels shouted at the press. They argued, like the Soviets, that "true freedom and objectivity are possible only in the service of a great cause." But they never

reached the level of totalitarianism which would have made the entire press a real instrument of the Nazi Party and government.

5. The Nazi concept of "the political type" contrasts interestingly with the "Bolshevik type," about which we have had something to say in the preceding pages. The Nazis said that a resurgent Germany required the creation of a "political type" "fashioned after the model of the leader (Hitler) and racially selected according to certain guiding principles." "The formation of this type must be attempted with all means available for the shaping of public opinion" (92). Like the Soviets, the Nazis brushed aside the concept of a free and spontaneous public opinion. Like the Soviets they rewrote the history books and the political textbooks, and like the Soviets they depended on the generation of youth to produce most of the desired "political type." It is interesting to see these two systems come out with essentially the same idea: that the mass communication instrument must mold citizens into the nation-instrument.

6. Finally, it should be pointed out that on both sides there has been a considerable amount of Prometheanism. The Party leaders in Russia have taken on themselves an almost frightening responsibility for giving 200 million people the "Right Line," permitting neither deviation nor discussion, and banking all the resources of the Union on the rightness of their perception. The Nazis also sought to create a new nation in the image of "the leader." They reinterpreted history. In fact, they staked all of Germany's resources on their new interpretation. In neither case were the Promethean leaders hesitant about sacrificing vast numbers of men on the altar of their belief — although one worshipped the somewhat irrational and misty deity of Kant, Fichte, Hegel, and Hitler, and the other the down-to-earth materialist, but in some respects equally irrational, deity of Marx, Engels, Lenin, and Stalin.

THE SOVIET CONCEPT AND OUR OWN

And finally, what shall we say of the relation of the Soviet concept and system to our own?

The question is rather, what should we add; for we have referred to this comparison through this paper, and our system has been quite fully explicated earlier in this volume.

The concepts and systems are so unlike, as we have tried to point out, that it is hard for people brought up in them to find common ground even to talk about them. The philosophies behind the two systems are vastly different — on the one side, Marxist materialistic determinism and class struggle; on the other, the rationalistic, natural rights philosophy of the Enlightenment. The concepts of man are wholly different — on the one side, man as a mass, malleable, unimportant in himself, in need of Promethean leadership; on the other side, man as intelligent, discriminating, perfectly able to purchase by himself in a "free market place of ideas." The concepts of the state are nearly opposite — on the one hand, an elected democracy conceived of as governing best when governing least; on the other, a self-appointed dictatorship, conceived of as "caretakers" of the people against untrue or misleading ideas. The concepts of truth are correspondingly different — on the one hand, something to be arrived at by argument and confrontation of evidence; on the other, something to be derived by straining events through a ready-made theoretical sieve. The concept of control is likewise wholly different — on the one side, extreme and complete control by ownership, Party membership, directives, censorship, review, criticism, and coercion; on the other side, the self-righting process of truth in the free market place, with the tiniest minimum of government controls. On the one side, there is a heavy emphasis on responsibility; on the other, on freedom. And the difference in basic concept is never better illustrated than by the picture of both systems going forward under the banners of "freedom," although by that term they mean quite different things.

But if we were to select two differences from the long list, and put them at the end of this paper, to be remembered, I think we should choose the following two.

In the first place, we should remind ourselves that basically the differences between the Soviet tradition and ours are the differences between Marx and Mill. Both these philosophers were concerned with the greatest good of the greatest number. But Marx would improve man by improving society — indeed, would use man as an engine to improve society to improve man. Mill, on the other hand, would improve society by first improving man. And so throughout the two traditions we have parallel but opposite concepts. On the Soviet side, they have to do with improving society: the rights of the working *class*, the classless *society*, etc. On our side, they have to do with improving the lot of the individual: the rights of *man, individual* freedom, etc.

In the second place, I think we should recall that in the Soviet

Union mass communication is essentially an instrument to be played upon, by direction of a few Promethean leaders, for a preset result. In our system, mass communication is a service rather than an instrument, and is used — not for preconceived ends — but rather as the voice of social and public needs, interests, tastes, and ideas, as observed and interpreted by the owners and managers of the media, for the purpose of selling a useful product. To Soviet observers, our media are therefore irresponsible and disorderly. To us, the Soviet mass media are "kept" and "servile." To the Soviets, the multidirectional quality, the openness, the unchecked criticism and conflict in our media represent a weakness in our national armor. To us, they seem our greatest strength. The next few decades will tell which is the better estimate.

BIBLIOGRAPHY

1. THE AUTHORITARIAN THEORY

Modern writers have produced very few expressions of the theory of authoritarianism. For the basic ideas underlying the practices of authoritarian and totalitarian governments, one must go to the writings of such philosophers as Plato, Hobbes, Hegel, Treitschke, Machiavelli as well as Rousseau, Carlyle, and Troeltsch.

The writings of Hitler and Mussolini and their apologists contain much material on the theoretical basis as well as on the practical workings of authoritarian principles.

Many of the books listed below contain bibliographies.

1. Boswell, James, *Boswell's Life of Johnson.* Edited by G. B. Hill, revised and edited by L. F. Powell; Oxford: Clarendon Press, 1934. Vol. 2.

2. Brown, Robert U., "IAPA Vows to Fight Political Oppression," *Editor & Publisher,* 88 (April 2, 1954) 12.

3. Catlin, George, *The Story of the Political Philosophers.* New York: Tudor Publishing Co., 1939.

4. Catlin, George, "Thomas Hobbes," in Edwin R. A. Seligman, editor, *Encyclopedia of the Social Sciences.* New York: Macmillan Co., 1935. Vol. 7.

5. Childs, Harwood L., and John B. Whitton, *Propaganda by Short Wave.* Princeton: Princeton University Press, 1942.

6. Ebenstein, William, *Man and the State.* New York: Rinehart and Co., 1947.

7. Fuller, B. A. G., *A History of Philosophy.* Revised edition; New York: Henry Holt and Co., 1945.

8. Harley, John E., *World-Wide Influences of the Cinema.* Los Angeles: University of Southern California Press, 1940.

9. Hitler, Adolph, *Mein Kampf.* Boston: Houghton Mifflin Co., 1937.

10. Hobbes, Thomas, *Leviathan.* New York: E. P. Dutton and Co., 1950.

11. Johnson, Samuel, *Lives of the English Poets.* Edited by G. B. Hill; Oxford: Clarendon Press, 1905. Vol. 1.

12. Kiefer, Alexander F., "Government Control of Publishing in Germany," *Political Science Quarterly*, 57 (March 1942) 73-97.

13. Krieg, Ugo, *La Legislazione Penale Sulla Stampi: Manuale Teorico-Practico.* Milano: A. Guiffrè, 1942.

14. Lopez, Salvador P., *Freedom of Information, 1953.* Report submitted to United Nations Economic and Social Council. New York, 1953. (Its Official Records, 16th Session. Suppl. no. 12.) Doc. E/2426.

15. MacIver, Robert M., *The Web of Government.* New York: Macmillan Co., 1947.

16. Mussolini, Benito, *The Political and Social Doctrine of Fascism.* English translation; London: Hogarth Press, 1933. Quoted in William Ebenstein, *Man and the State.* New York: Rinehart and Co., 1947, pp. 303-04.

17. New York *Times,* July 5, 1954, p. 10, col. 2.

18. New York *Times,* Dec. 25, 1955, p. 4, col. 1.

19. Political and Economic Planning, *The British Film Industry.* London: P E P (Political and Economic Planning), 1952.

20. *Rex vs. Tutchin,* 14 State Trials (1704).

21. Shepard, W. J., "Government. History and Theory," in Seligman, editor, *Encyclopedia of the Social Sciences.* Vol. 7.

22. Siebert, Fredrick Seaton, *Freedom of the Press in England 1476-1776.* Urbana: University of Illinois Press, 1952.

23. Sington, Derrick, and Arthur Weidenfeld, *The Goebbels Experiment: A Study of the Nazi Propaganda Machine.* London: John Murray, 1943.

24. Stephen, Sir James Fitzjames, *History of the Criminal Law of England.* London: Macmillan Co., 1883. Vol. 2.

25. Stephen, Sir James Fitzjames, *Liberty, Equality, Fraternity.* New York: Henry Holt and Co., 1882.

26. United Nations, *Yearbook on Human Rights for 1952.* New York: United Nations, 1954.

27. Williamson, George Ed, "IPI Vows Full Publicity Attack on Press Enemies," *Editor & Publisher,* 88 (May 21, 1955) 74.

28. Zimmern, Alfred, editor, *Modern Political Doctrines.* New York: Oxford University Press, 1939.

2. THE LIBERTARIAN THEORY

29. Antieau, Chester, " 'Clear and Present Danger' — Its Meaning and Significance," *Notre Dame Lawyer,* 25 (Summer 1950) 604-45.

30. Antieau, Chester, "The Rule of Clear and Present Danger; Scope of Its Applicability," *Michigan Law Review*, 48 (April 1950) 811-40.

31. Becker, Carl L., *Freedom and Responsibility in the American Way of Life.* New York: Alfred A. Knopf, 1945.

32. Becker, Carl L., *New Liberties for Old.* New Haven: Yale University Press, 1941.

33. Becker, Carl L., *Progress and Power.* New York: Alfred A. Knopf, 1949.

34. Blackstone, Sir William, *Commentaries on the Law of England.* Chicago: Callaghan, 1899. Vol. 2, Bk. iv, Sec. 152.

35. Brucker, Herbert, *Freedom of Information.* New York: Macmillan Co., 1949.

36. *Burstyn vs. Wilson,* 72 S. Ct. 777 (1952).

37. Cassirer, Ernst, "Enlightenment," in Edwin R. A. Seligman, editor, *Encyclopedia of the Social Sciences.* New York: Macmillan Co., 1935. Vol. 5.

38. "Censorship of Motion Pictures," *Yale Law Journal,* 49 (November 1939) 87-113.

39. Chafee, Zechariah, Jr., *Freedom of Speech in the United States.* Cambridge: Harvard University Press, 1941.

40. Chafee, Zechariah, Jr., *Government and Mass Communications.* Chicago: University of Chicago Press, 1947. 2 vols.

41. Chenery, William L., *Freedom of the Press.* New York: Harcourt, Brace and Co., 1955.

42. Cross, Harold L., *The People's Right to Know.* New York: Columbia University Press, 1953.

43. Editorial, "El Tiempo," *Editor & Publisher,* 88 (Aug. 13, 1955) 36.

44. Gerald, J. Edward, *The Press and the Constitution 1931-1947.* Minneapolis: University of Minnesota Press, 1948.

45. Gildersleeve, Virginia Crocheron, *Government Regulation of Elizabethan Drama.* New York: Columbia University Press, 1908.

46. Howell, Thomas B., compiler, *A Complete Collection of State Trials.* London: 1704. Vol. 22. (Erskine's defense of Paine for publishing *The Rights of Man.*)

47. Inglis, Ruth, *Freedom of the Movies.* Chicago: University of Chicago Press, 1947.

48. Jefferson, Thomas, *The Writings of Thomas Jefferson.* Edited by Andrew A. Lipscomb; Memorial edition; Washington, D.C.: Thomas Jefferson Memorial Association, 1904. Vol. 11.

49. Laski, Harold J., *The Rise of European Liberalism.* London: G. Allen and Unwin Ltd., 1936.

50. Lopez, Salvador P., *Freedom of Information, 1953.* Report submitted to United Nations Economic and Social Council. New York, 1953. (Its Official Records, 16th Session. Suppl. no. 12.) Doc. E/2426.

51. Meiklejohn, Alexander, *Free Speech and Its Relation to Self-Government.* New York: Harper and Brothers, 1948.

52. Mill, John Stuart, *On Liberty.* Edited by Alburey Castell; New York: F. S. Crofts and Co., 1947.

53. Milton, John, *Areopagitica.* Edited by George H. Sabine; New York: Appleton-Century-Crofts, 1951.

54. Mock, James R., *Censorship, 1917.* Princeton: Princeton University Press, 1941.

55. Mott, Frank L., *Jefferson and the Press.* Baton Rouge: Louisiana State University Press, 1943.

56. National Association of Broadcasters, *Broadcasting and the Bill of Rights. Statements Prepared by Representatives of the Broadcasting Industry on the WHITE BILL (S. 1333) to Amend the Communications Act of 1934.* Washington, D.C., 1947.

57. *Schenck vs. United States,* 249 U.S. 47 (1919).

58. Siebert, Fredrick Seaton, *Freedom of the Press in England 1476-1776.* Urbana: University of Illinois Press, 1952.

59. United Nations Conference on Freedom of Information, Geneva, 1948 — Delegates from the United States, *Report of the United States Delegates with Related Documents.* Washington, D.C.: Government Printing Office, 1948.

60. U.S. — Federal Communications Commission, *Public Service Responsibility of Broadcast Licensees.* (Blue Book) Washington, D.C., 1946.

61. Waples, Douglas, editor, *Print, Radio and Film in a Democracy.* Chicago: University of Chicago Press, 1942.

62. White, Llewellyn, *The American Radio.* Chicago: University of Chicago Press, 1947.

63. Willey, Malcolm M., and Ralph D. Casey, editors, "The Press in the Contemporary Scene," *Annals of the American Academy of Political and Social Science,* 219 (January 1942).

64. Yeager, W. Hayes, and William Utterback, editors, "Communication and Social Action," *Annals of the American Academy of Political and Social Science,* 250 (March 1947).

3. THE SOCIAL RESPONSIBILITY THEORY

For a presentation of social responsibility theory as developed by the Commission on Freedom of the Press, the best sources obviously are the reports sponsored by the Commission (items 65, 66, 69, 70, 81). Most important is *A Free and Responsible Press.* Hocking's book is an excellent companion volume, since it enlarges upon many of the principles on which the joint work is based. Those two books give an adequate expression of the Commission's ideas, but Chafee's two volumes also are worth special attention. No single work pulls together social responsibility theory as it is being developed by the press itself. However, such periodicals as *Nieman Reports* and *Quill* regularly carry articles in which practitioners discuss their duties to the public.

65. Chafee, Zechariah, Jr., *Government and Mass Communications.* Chicago: University of Chicago Press, 1947. 2 vols.

66. Commission on Freedom of the Press, *A Free and Responsible Press.* Chicago: University of Chicago Press, 1947.

67. Davis, Elmer, *But We Were Born Free.* Indianapolis: Bobbs-Merrill Co., 1954.

68. General Council of the Press, *The Press and the People.* London: General Council of the Press, 1954.

69. Hocking, William Ernest, *Freedom of the Press: A Framework of Principle.* Chicago: University of Chicago Press, 1947.

70. Inglis, Ruth, *Freedom of the Movies.* Chicago: University of Chicago Press, 1947.

71. Irwin, Will, "The American Newspaper," a series of fifteen articles in *Collier's* between Jan. 21, 1911, and July 29, 1911.

72. Isaacs, Norman, "A Small Town Paper Has One Supreme Ethical Duty — To Print the News," *Quill,* 41 (December 1953) 7-8, 15-16.

73. Jensen, Jay W., "Toward a Solution of the Problem of Freedom of the Press," *Journalism Quarterly,* 27 (Fall 1950) 399-408.

74. National Association of Radio and Television Broadcasters, *The Television Code.* Washington, D.C.: National Association of Radio and Television Broadcasters, 1954.

75. Pulitzer, Joseph, "The College of Journalism," *North American Review,* 178 (May 1904) 641-80.

76. Royal Commission on the Press, 1947-49, *Report.* London: His Majesty's Stationery Office, 1949.

77. *St. Louis Post-Dispatch Symposium on Freedom of the Press.* St. Louis: The Post-Dispatch, 1938.

78. Schramm, Wilbur, editor, *Mass Communications.* Urbana: University of Illinois Press, 1949. "Canons of Journalism," "The Broadcaster's Creed," "The Movies Production Code," 236-56.

79. Svirsky, Leon, editor, *Your Newspaper: Blueprint for a Better Press.* New York: Macmillan Co., 1947.

80. U.S. — Federal Communications Commission, *Fifteenth Annual Report.* Washington, D.C., 1949.

81. White, Llewellyn, *The American Radio.* Chicago: University of Chicago Press, 1947.

82. Whitehead, Alfred North, *Science and the Modern World.* New York: New American Library, 1948.

4. THE SOVIET COMMUNIST THEORY

Just as the works of Marx, Lenin, and Stalin are the basic texts for filling in the background of this subject, so also it is necessary to indicate two contemporary books to which this paper is in debt and, indeed, without the use of which it would be a much more difficult task to write the Soviet concept of the press. One of these is Andrei Vyshinsky's *Law of the Soviet State,* which explicates the Soviet viewpoint. The other is Alex Inkeles' *Public Opinion in Soviet Russia,* which is the most complete and impressive treatment we have of the Soviet mass media. Too late to cite or make use of in this paper have appeared a noteworthy volume by Raymond A. Bauer, Alex Inkeles, and Clyde W. Kluckhohn, entitled *How the Soviet System Works* (Cambridge: Harvard University Press, 1956) and an insightful paper by Paul Kecskemeti, "The Soviet Approach to International Political Communication," (POQ, Spring 1956). Among the works used and in many cases referred to in this paper are:

83. Barghoorn, Frederick C., *The Soviet Image of the United States.* New York: Harcourt, Brace and Co., 1950.

84. Bauer, Raymond A., *The New Man in Soviet Psychology.* Cambridge: Harvard University Press, 1952.

85. Brinton, Crane, *The Shaping of the Modern Mind.* New York: New American Library, 1953.

86. *Constitution of the Union of Soviet Socialist Republics.* Moscow: Foreign Language Publishing House, 1947.

87. Crossman, Richard, editor, *The God That Failed.* New York: Bantam Books, 1952.

88. Domenach, Jean-Marie, "Leninist Propaganda," *Public Opinion Quarterly,* 15 (Summer 1951) 265-73.

89. Engels, Friedrich, *Writings.* New York, 1915-21.

90. Fainsod, Merle, *How Russia Is Ruled.* Cambridge: Harvard University Press, 1953.

91. Farago, Ladislav, "Soviet Propaganda," *United Nations World* (September 1948) 18-24.

92. Hadamovsky, Eugen, *Propaganda und National Macht.* Oldenburg, 1933.

93. *History of the Communist Party of the Soviet Union* (Bolsheviks). Short Course. New York: International Publishers, 1939.

94. Hook, Sidney, *International Communism.* Montgomery, Ala.: U.S. Air Force, 1952.

95. Inkeles, Alex, *Public Opinion in Soviet Russia,* Cambridge: Harvard University Press, 1950.

96. Kecskemeti, Paul, "Totalitarian Communication as a Means of Control," *Public Opinion Quarterly,* 14 (Summer 1950) 224-34.

97. Kelsen, Hans, *The Political Theory of Bolshevism*. Berkeley and Los Angeles: University of California Press, 1949.
98. Kennan, George F., *American Diplomacy 1900-1950*. New York: New American Library, 1952. (Includes the well-known paper by "X" from *Foreign Affairs*.)
99. Lasswell, Harold D., "The Strategy of Soviet Propaganda," *Proceedings of the Academy of Political Science*, 24, 214-226.
100. Leites, Nathan, *A Study of Bolshevism*. Glencoe, Ill.: The Free Press, 1953.
101. Leites, Nathan, *The Operational Code of the Politburo*. New York: McGraw-Hill, 1951.
102. Lenin, Vladimir Ilyich, *Collected Works*. New York: International Publishers, 1927.
103. Marx, Karl, *Capital*. Chicago: Kerr, 1909.
104. Mead, Margaret, *Soviet Attitudes Toward Authority*. New York: McGraw-Hill, 1951.
105. Muller, Herbert, *The Uses of the Past*. New York: Oxford University Press, 1952.
106. Nemzer, Louis, "The Kremlin's Professional Staff," *American Political Science Review*, 44 (1950) 64-85.
107. Peters, J., *The Communist Party — A Manual on Organization*. New York: Workers Library, 1935.
108. Plekhanov, G. B., *Sochineniya* (Works). Moscow: Gosudarstvennoe Izdatel'stvo, 1927.
109. Rostow, W. W., *The Dynamics of Soviet Society*. Cambridge, Mass.: Technology Press, 1952.
110. Schramm, Wilbur, *The Soviet Concept of "Psychological" Warfare*. Washington, D.C.: USIA, 1955.
111. Schramm, Wilbur, and John W. Riley, Jr., "Communication in the Sovietized State as Represented in Korea," *American Sociological Review*, 16 (1951) 757-66.
112. Selznick, Philip, *The Organizational Weapon: A Study of Bolshevik Strategy and Tactics*. New York: McGraw-Hill, 1952.
113. Stalin, Joseph, *Problems of Leninism*. Moscow: Foreign Language Publishing House, 1940.
114. Stalin, Joseph, *Sochineniya* (Works). Moscow: State Publishing House, 1946-52.
115. Trotsky, Leon, *History of the Russian Revolution*. New York: Simon and Schuster, 1932.
116. Vyshinsky, Andrei, *The Law of the Soviet State*. New York: Macmillan Co., 1948.

UNIVERSITY OF ILLINOIS PRESS
1325 SOUTH OAK STREET
CHAMPAIGN, ILLINOIS 61820-6903
WWW.PRESS.UILLINOIS.EDU